Mountain Biking
The White
Mountains
WEST

J. RICHARD DURNAN

FALCON® Helena, Montana

A FALCON GUIDE®

Falcon® Publishing is continually expanding its list of recreational guide-books. All books include detailed descriptions, accurate maps, and all the information necessary for enjoyable trips. You can order extra copies of this book and get information and prices for other Falcon guidebooks by writing Falcon, P.O. Box 1718, Helena, MT 59624 or calling toll free 1-800-582-2665. Also, please ask for a free copy of our current catalog. Visit our website at http:\\www.falconguide.com

©1998 by Falcon® Publishing, Inc., Helena, Montana.
Printed in Canada.

1 2 3 4 5 6 7 8 9 0 TP 03 02 01 00 99 98

Falcon and FalconGuide are registered trademarks of Falcon® Publishing, Inc.

Cover photo by J. Richard Durnan.

Library of Congress Cataloging-in-Publication Data

J. Richard Durnan
    Mountain biking the White Mountains (west) / by J. Richard Durnan.
        p.   cm.
    ISBN 1-56044-663-3 (pbk.)
    1. All terrain cycling—White Mountains (N.H. and Me.)—Guidebooks.
    2. White Mountains (N.H. and Me.)—Guidebooks.
  I. Title.
GV1045.5.W55D87   1998
917.42 ' 20443—dc21

                             98-6249
                               CIP

CAUTION
Outdoor recreational activities are by their very nature potentially hazardous. All participants in such activities must assume the responsibility for their own actions and safety. The information contained in this guidebook cannot re-place sound judgment and good decision-making skills, which help reduce the risk exposure, nor does the scope of this book allow for disclosure of all the potential hazards and risks involved in such activities.
    Learn as much as possible about the outdoor recreational activities in which you participate, prepare for the unexpected, and be cautious. The re-ward will be a safer and more enjoyable experience.

 Text pages printed on recycled paper.

Contents

Foreword

Welcome to the most up-to-date mountain bike guide available detailing the trails and backroads of the western White Mountain region of New Hampshire. I have had the pleasure of exploring most of the rides described in this guide during my thirteen years of living in the Plymouth area. Mountain bikers from beginner to expert will find this guide to be a concise and easy-to-use reference tool.

I would like to emphasize that many of these rides utilize historically significant byways, following old logging roads and railbeds which pass by colonial-era stone walls and foundations built by New Hampshire's original settlers. You'll see evidence of this everywhere; take a moment to use your imagination and wonder about the challenges and hardships that were faced by these rugged people. Certainly, their daily lives were far more difficult than what we face today when we're grinding uphill in pursuit of cycling nirvana!

Please respect the rights of private property owners and do not trespass. Also, try to avoid riding trails when they are wet and prone to erosion. Many individuals and organizations volunteer their time and energy to maintain these trails; please keep this in mind when you encounter a tree across a trail and are presented with the choice of riding around it or taking a moment to dismount and remove the hazard.

I'd also like to stress the importance of being thoroughly prepared when entering the White Mountains. Most of these trails access true backcountry and require that you come equipped to handle any mechanical breakdowns or medical emergencies on your own. New Hampshire is famous for its constantly changing weather, so even if it's sunny and warm when you start out, be prepared for extreme conditions during the course of your outing.

Local bike shops are usually your best source for current information about trail conditions and additional riding opportunities in each region, so be sure to stop in and chat it up before hitting the trails. Above all, please enjoy and respect the diverse and challenging beauty of mountain biking in the White Mountains.

Slade Warner
Rhino Bikes

Acknowledgments

If you ever come across a guidebook without this section, throw it away! I cannot imagine completing, or even beginning, a task such as this without the support and help that I have received. My thanks to everyone who helped me in ways big and small.

Endless thanks to my longtime and unconditional friends Suzanne and Duane Snell. Thank you for letting me set up mountain-bike base camp in your home. The camper in the driveway (my home away from home) was perfect, and so were the great meals. I could not have finished this project without all the support you both gave me. It's done now, and you can have your computer back.

Bally Thune, thanks for the hours of editing you gave to this manuscript, and to all the fun nights up on "The Hill" with you and Bobby when I needed to get away from riding and writing.

For all the invaluable local information, and for keeping my bike in good shape, thanks to Tim Gotwols, at Riverside Cycles, and to Slade Warner. Thanks also to Vince Bell at White Mountain Cyclists for the trail tips in your backyard.

It was great riding with you, Scot Christenson. Thanks for sharing your favorite trails and your knowledge of the local lore. The maps taken off your dining room table were invaluable.

Andy Richmond, you were great company on the trail. Thanks for the hours of adventure and your patience for me and my camera.

It's not an easy task to review a manuscript. Thanks to Slade Warner at Rhino Bikes, to Bob Spoerl at the New Hampshire Trails Bureau, and to District Ranger Anne Archie of the Pemigewasset Ranger District.

Finally, thanks to Sarah Snyder for getting me interested in this project and helping me to make all the right connections.

Thanks, Mom and Dad, for your support while I chase my dreams.

MAP LEGEND

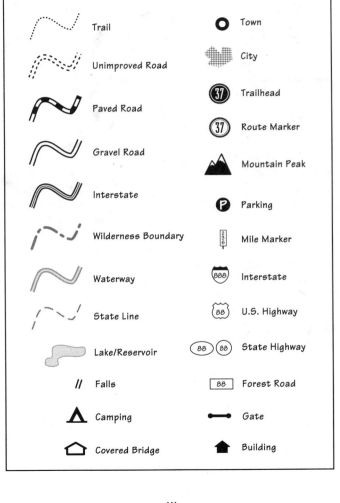

- Trail
- Unimproved Road
- Paved Road
- Gravel Road
- Interstate
- Wilderness Boundary
- Waterway
- State Line
- Lake/Reservoir
- // Falls
- Camping
- Covered Bridge

- Town
- City
- (37) Trailhead
- (37) Route Marker
- Mountain Peak
- (P) Parking
- Mile Marker
- (888) Interstate
- (88) U.S. Highway
- (88) (88) State Highway
- [88] Forest Road
- Gate
- Building

USGS
TOPO MAP

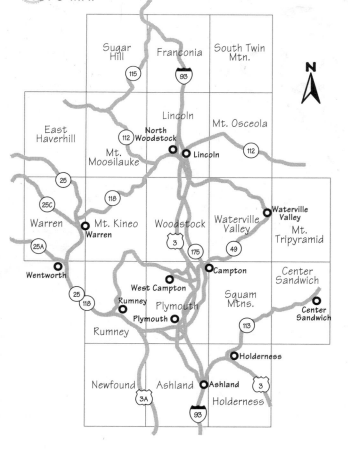

ix

OVERVIEW MAP

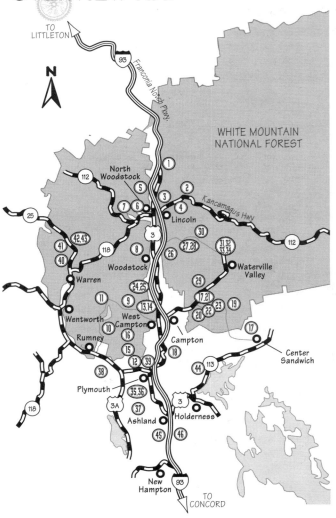

Get Ready to CRANK!

To include every ride in an area as diverse as New Hampshire's western White Mountains and the Pemigewasset (Pemi) River Valley would not only be impossible to do but would take away the fun of discovering them for yourself. Whether you're a local or a visitor to the area, before the fun begins you need to decide where to ride. There is no end to your options, which range from scenic cruises to lung-bustin' technical hill climbs and descents.

Mountain Biking the White Mountains is a guide that gives you an introduction to some of the more classic rides in the area. It can be stuffed in your bike bag and used to provide a detailed outline of the ride or just to steer you in the direction of a ride you have never done before.

The rides described in this guide are written in plain language and provide distances and ratings for physical and technical difficulty so you can know what you're getting into before you actually get into it. The aim is threefold: to help you choose a ride that's appropriate for your fitness and skill level; to make it easy to find the trailhead; and to help you complete the ride safely, without getting lost. Take care of the basics and you will have a great experience.

The White Mountains: What to Expect

The rides in this book are found in New Hampshire's Pemigewasset River drainage, an area extending from Ashland in the south to Franconia Notch—where the headwaters of the Pemigewasset River are located—in the north. Most of this area is in the mountains and a large part is located within the boundaries of White Mountain National Forest, which is a little larger than Rhode Island. Many of the trails are old logging roads or abandoned logging railway beds, a product of New Hampshire's logging days, which are now part of its rich history. Active logging in the area is also responsible for an ever-increasing number of new and changing trails.

Being Prepared: Expect and be prepared for anything and everything that can happen in the mountains. You will be subject to mountain weather conditions and terrain. Always be prepared with warm clothing and rain gear.

Terrain: The terrain you will ride features shady, forested, muddy, and often steep and technical trails. Most of the out-and-back rides climb going out and descend on the return. Rivers and streams on New Hampshire trails often may have to be crossed without bridges. During the spring runoff, stream crossings you rode another time may be uncrossable. Don't plan a ride with a potentially hazardous crossing when water levels are known to be high. Recognize your limits and use common sense.

Weather: The best riding is from late spring to fall. New Hampshire enjoys warm summer days with cool nights. Average temperatures in July are 81 degrees F (high) and 53 degrees F (low). Average annual rainfall in Plymouth is 38 inches. The winters are long and snowy. The average temperature in January is 15 degrees F. Up to 90 inches of snow fall in Plymouth, more in the mountains. Still, a few diehards who can't put their bikes away get out for rides in the winter with studded tires on the icy, snowpacked trails. Rides on plowed back roads are perhaps a more conventional option. Complete weather forecasts are available at ranger stations (see Appendix B).

New Hampshire actually has five seasons: spring, summer, fall, winter, and "mud and bug" season, which overlaps spring and summer.

Trails and roads are muddy from when the snowpack begins to melt until late spring. If you don't like getting muddy, you picked the wrong state. Mud characterizes the riding in New Hampshire. Be kind to the trails during mud season. Avoid known muddy or fragile trails and carry bikes around, rather than riding through, mud holes. Damage done riding trails with fat tires only makes it harder for those who follow, both physically and politically.

The "wicked" bugs, including mosquitoes and the infamous New Hampshire blackflies, are usually at their worst from mid-May to mid-June and are gone, hopefully, by early July. You will find the heaviest clouds of bugs descending on you when you're near water, particularly standing water in marshes. However, these bugs provide excellent incentive to keep riding even through the most difficult terrain. Bug repellent is an excellent addition to your kit; some consider it essential.

Water: Don't forget to take water! Particularly on hot summer days, your body will thank you for providing lots of it. Drinking between 1.5 and 2.5 gallons of water each day is recommended. Although it is tempting to grab a gulp of water from a (presumably) clean, fresh, cool mountain stream, it is not recommended. Surface waters can contain cysts and parasites, such as the infamous *Giardia*. If you can't carry enough water for the day, bring something to treat it. The best method, boiling, is probably out, so try iodine or chlorine-based treatments and filters. Carry at least one bottle of water and/or a treatment. There are some really great "hydration" pack systems available that hold a lot of water comfortably.

Trail Maintenance: There are no trail fairies in New Hampshire that do trail maintenance. Organizations such as the Appalachian Mountain Club (AMC), Squam Lakes Association (SLA), and local snowmobile clubs do a lot of the work. Respect their efforts and contribute when you can. Take the time to clear a log or fill in a mud hole. A little sweat for the trail will keep you sweating on the trail.

That said, many people do work that they feel helps but actually does harm. Before setting out to maintain a trail on your own, seek out an experienced group to gain work experience with first.

IMBA Rules of the Trail

Keep trails open by setting a good example of environmentally sound and socially responsible off-road cycling. Thousands of miles of dirt trails have been closed to mountain bikers. The irresponsible riding habits of a few riders have been a factor. Do your part to maintain trail access by observing the following rules of the trail, formulated by the International Mountain Bicycling Association (IMBA). IMBA's mission is to promote environmentally sound and socially responsible mountain biking.

1. Ride on open trails only. Respect trail and road closures (ask if not sure), avoid possible trespass on private land, and obtain permits and authorization as may be required. Federal and state wilderness areas are closed to cycling. The way you ride will influence trail management decisions and policies.

2. Leave no trace. Be sensitive to the dirt beneath you. Even on open (legal) trails, you should not ride under conditions where you will leave evidence of your passing, such as on certain soils after a rain. Recognize different types of soil and trail construction; practice low-impact cycling. This also means staying on existing trails and not creating any new ones. Be sure to pack out at least as much as you pack in.

3. Control your bicycle! Inattention for even a second can cause problems. Obey all bicycle speed regulations and recommendations.

4. Always yield trail. Make known your approach well in advance. A friendly greeting (or bell) is considerate and works well; don't startle others. Show your respect when passing by slowing to a walking pace or even stopping. Anticipate other trail users around corners and blind spots.

5. Never spook animals. All animals are startled by an unannounced approach, a sudden movement, or a loud noise. This can be dangerous for you, others, and the animals. Give animals extra room and time to adjust to you. When passing horses, use special care and follow directions from the horseback riders (dismount and move to the downhill side of the trail if uncertain). Running cattle and disturbing wildlife is a serious offense. Leave gates as you found them or as marked.

6. Plan ahead. Know your equipment, your ability, and the area in which you are riding—and prepare accordingly. Be self-sufficient at all times, keep your equipment in good repair, and carry necessary supplies for changes in weather or other conditions. A well-executed trip is a satisfaction to you and not a burden or offense to others. Always wear a helmet.

How to Use This Guide

Mountain Biking the White Mountains (West) describes forty-six mountain bike rides. When possible, I have described the rides as loops to keep you constantly challenged by new terrain, yet let you begin and end in the same place. Be forewarned, however: the difficulty of a loop ride may change dramatically depending on which direction you ride around the loop. If you are unfamiliar with the rides in this book, try them first as described here. The directions follow the path of least resistance (which does not necessarily mean "easy"). After you've been over the terrain, you can determine whether a given loop would be fun—or even feasible—in the reverse direction.

Those rides that are not described as loops are out-and-back rides. However, they are only described going out. To return, you simply return the way you came and follow the directions backwards.

Portions of some rides follow gravel and even paved roads, and a handful of rides never wander off road. Purists may wince at road rides in a mountain-biking guide, but these are special rides. They offer a chance to enjoy mountain scenery and fresh air while covering easier, non-technical terrain for people new to the sport. They can also be used by the hard-core riders on "active rest" days or when the off-road trails are out of shape with mud or snow.

Each ride description in this book follows the same format:

Number and name of the ride: Rides are cross-referenced by number throughout the book. In many cases, parts of rides or entire routes can be linked to other rides for longer trips or variations on a standard route. These opportunities are noted with a reference to the ride number: "Ride(s) XX."

For the names of rides, I relied on official names of trails, roads, and natural features shown on National Forest and U.S. Geological Survey (USGS) maps. In some cases, deference was given to long-term local custom.

Location: The general whereabouts of the ride, distance, and direction are given from an Interstate 93 exit, beginning at the end of the northbound off ramp.

Distance: The length of the ride in miles, given as a loop, a one way, or a round trip.

Time: An estimate of how long it takes to complete the ride, for example, 1 to 2 hours. *The time listed is the actual riding time and does not include rest stops.* Strong, skilled riders may be able to do a given ride in less than the estimated time, while other riders may take considerably longer. Bear in mind that severe weather, changes in the trail conditions, or mechanical problems may prolong a ride.

Tread: The type of road or trail: paved road, gravel road, dirt road or jeep trail, doubletrack, All-terrain-vehicle-width singletrack, and singletrack.

Aerobic level: The level of physical effort required to complete the ride: easy, moderate, or strenuous (see Rating the Rides).

Technical difficulty: The level of bike-handling skills needed to complete the ride upright and in one piece. Technical difficulty is rated on a scale of 1 to 5, with 1 being the easiest and 5 the hardest (see Rating the Rides).

Highlights: Special features or qualities that make a ride worthwhile (as if we need an excuse!): scenery, fun singletrack, chances to see wildlife, etc.

Hazards: A list of dangers that may be encountered on a ride, including traffic, weather, trail obstacles and poor conditions, risky stream crossings, obscure trails, and other perils. Remember: conditions may change at any time. Be alert for storms, new fences, downfall, missing trail signs, and mechanical failure. Fatigue, heat, cold, and/or dehydration may impair judgment. Always wear a helmet and other safety equipment. Ride in control at all times.

Land status: A list of managing agencies or landowners. Many of the rides in this book are in the White Mountain National Forest. All trails in the national forest are open to mountain biking except those that lie in officially designated wilderness areas (36 Code of Federal Regulations, CFR, 261.16) or any part of the Appalachian National Scenic Trail (36 CFR 261.55 (b)). Some of the rides also cross portions of private, state, or municipal lands. Always leave gates as you found them, and respect the land, regardless of who owns it. (See Appendix B for local addresses of land-managing agencies.)

Maps: A list of available maps. The White Mountain National Forest (WMNF) Mountain Bike Map is an excellent 1:63, 360 scale map that shows many of the rides in this book that are within the White Mountain National Forest boundaries. The USGS maps in the 7.5-minute series are also very good sources and are the basis for the WMNF Mountain Bike Map and this book's maps.

Access: How to find the trailhead or the start of the ride. All directions begin from an Interstate 93 exit.

The ride: A mile-by-mile list of key points—landmarks, notable climbs and descents, stream crossings, obstacles, hazards, major turns, and junctions along the ride. All distances were measured to the tenth of a mile with a cyclo-computer (a bike-mounted odometer). Terrain, riding technique, and even tire pressure can affect odometer readings, so treat all mileages as estimates.

A final reminder: The real world is changing all the time. The information presented here is as accurate and up-to-date as possible, but there are no guarantees in the mountains. Logging, particularly, can drastically change the location and conditions of trails. You are responsible for your safety and for the choices you make on the trail. Talk to riders and to staff in local shops about changes, conditions, and new rides. If you find an error or omission in this book, or a new and noteworthy change in the field, I'd like to hear from you. Please write to Rich Durnan, c/o Falcon Publishing, P.O. Box 1718, Helena, MT 59624, or e-mail me at Falcon@desktop.org.

Rating the Rides

While I have tried to make all the ratings in this book relative to one another, a rating system of this nature is still very subjective. So, if a trail is rated a 3 in this book but you feel it deserves a 4, you can adjust the rating of the next ride to your ability—that is, you will know that the next 3 you set out to ride is likely to be a 4.

The following sections explain what the various ratings mean. An elevation profile accompanies each ride description to help you determine the ease or difficulty of the ride. When assessing a ride's ratings, always compute in such other factors as total trip distance, weather and wind, and current trail conditions.

Aerobic Level Ratings

Bicycling is often touted as a relaxing, low-impact, relatively easy way to burn excess calories and maintain a healthy heart and lungs. Mountain biking, however, tends to pack a little more work (and excitement) into the routine.

Fat tires and soft or rough trails increase the rolling resistance, so it takes more effort to push those wheels around. And unpaved or off-road hills tend to be steeper than grades measured and tarred by the highway department. When we use the word *steep*, we mean a sweat-inducing, oxygen-sucking, lactose-building climb. If it's followed by an exclamation point—steep(!)—expect some honest pain on the way up (and maybe for days afterward).

So expect to breathe hard and sweat some, probably a lot. Pedaling around town is a good start, but it won't fully prepare you for the workout offered by most of the rides in this book. If you're unsure of your level of fitness, see a doctor for a physical exam before tackling any of these rides. And if you're riding to get back in shape, or just for the fun of it, take it easy. Walk or rest if need be. Start with short rides and add miles gradually.

Here's how we rate the exertion level for terrain covered in this book:

Easy: Rides are mostly on flat or gently rolling terrain. No steep or prolonged climbs.

Moderate: Some hills. Climbs may be short and fairly steep or long and gradual.

9

Strenuous: Frequent or prolonged climbs steep enough to require riding in the lowest gear; requires a high level of aerobic fitness, power, and endurance (typically acquired through many hours of riding and proper training). Less fit riders may need to walk.

Elevation Graphs

An elevation profile accompanies each ride description. The profiles graph the ups and downs of each route on a grid of elevation (in feet above sea level) on the left and miles pedaled across the bottom. Route surface conditions or tread and technical levels are also shown on the graphs.

These graphs are compressed to fit on the printed page. The actual slopes you ride are not as steep as the lines drawn on the graphs (though they may feel that way). Some extremely short dips and climbs are too small to show up on the graphs. All abrupt changes in gradient are, however, mentioned in the mile-by-mile ride descriptions.

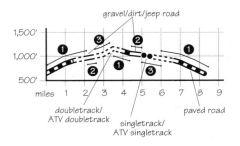

Technical Difficulty Ratings

Technical difficulty is rated on a scale of 1 to 5 (1 being easiest). The ratings have been made as objective as possible by considering the type and frequency of the ride's obstacles. The same standards were applied consistently for all rides in this book.

A plus (+) or minus (-) symbol is used to designate the difficulty ratings between each level of difficulty: for example, a 4+ is harder than a 4 but easier than a 5-. A stretch of trail rated as 5+ would be unrideable by all but the most skilled (or luckiest) riders.

Following are the five levels defined:

Level 1: Smooth tread; road or doubletrack; no obstacles, ruts, or steeps. Requires basic bike-riding skills.

Level 2: Mostly smooth tread; wide, well-groomed singletrack or road/doubletrack with minor ruts or loose gravel and sand.

Level 3: Irregular tread with some rough sections; single or doubletrack with obvious route choices; some steep sections; occasional obstacles may include small rocks, roots, water bars, ruts, loose gravel or sand, and sharp turns or broad, open switchbacks.

Level 4: Rough tread with few smooth places; singletrack or rough doubletrack with limited route choices; steep sections, some with obstacles; obstacles are numerous and varied, including rocks, roots, branches, ruts, sidehills, narrow tread, loose gravel or sand, and switchbacks.

Level 5: Continuously broken, rocky, root-infested, or trenched tread; singletrack or extremely rough doubletrack with few route choices; frequent or sudden and severe changes in gradient; some slopes so steep that wheels lift off the ground;

obstacles are nearly continuous and may include boulders, logs, water, large holes, deep ruts, ledges, piles of loose gravel, steep sidehills, encroaching trees, and tight switchbacks.

Lincoln

Franconia Notch Bike Path

Location: 0.1 mile east of Interstate 93 (Franconia Notch State Parkway), exit 1, in Franconia Notch State Park.

Distance: 6.9-mile one way.

Time: 30 minutes to 1.5 hours.

Tread: 6.9 miles on paved bike path.

Aerobic level: Easy.

Technical difficulty: 1 on paved bike trail.

Highlights: A well-marked, gently rolling ride crisscrossing the Pemigewasset River through Franconia Notch to its headwaters at Profile Lake. See the famous Old Man of the Mountain (he's there till late every night) and the Basin, a 30-foot-wide, 15-foot-deep pothole that Samuel Easton described in his 1958 *White Mountain Guide* as "...one of the beautiful haunts of nature. A luxurious and delicious bath fit for the ablutions of a goddess." This ride is popular with families and offers many excellent picnic spots.

Hazards: Pedestrians, chipmunks, and midget mice. They run out in front of you all the time!

Land status: Franconia Notch State Park.

Maps: Franconia Notch State Park Recreational Trail Map (available at the Flume Information Center); USGS Lincoln and Franconia Quadrangles (trail not shown).

Access: From Franconia Notch State Parkway (Interstate 93), follow signs to the Flume Gorge Park Information Center. Park in the parking lot and follow bike-route signs to the trailhead at the northernmost parking tier. The ride begins as you leave the parking lot where the pavement is painted with the words "Start Bike Route."

The ride

0.0 Follow the bike-route signs from the north end of the Flume Gorge visitor center parking area into a mixed hardwood forest on the paved bike path. Please note the path rules: Ride or walk bikes in single file, pedestrians yield to bikes, and the trail opens 30 minutes before sunrise and closes 30 minutes after sunset. Soon pass the Mount Pemigewasset–Indian Head Summit Trail on the left and continue past a stop sign.

0.9 Cross a bridge over the Pemigewasset River, past the Pemi Trail on the near side and the Liberty Springs Trail on the far side.

1.6 Walk your bike through the lower parking area for the Basin. The trail passes the bathrooms on the right; stay left and go under the parkway through a tunnel.

1.8 Pass a basin viewpoint on the left.

FRANCONIA NOTCH
BIKE PATH
Ride 1

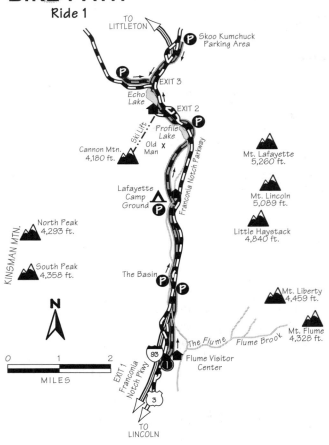

TO
LITTLETON

Skoo Kumchuck
Parking Area

EXIT 3

Echo
Lake

EXIT 2

Ski Lift

Profile
Lake

Old
Man

Cannon Mtn.
4,180 ft.

Mt. Lafayette
5,260 ft.

Lafayette
Camp
Ground

Franconia Notch Parkway

Mt. Lincoln
5,089 ft.

KINSMAN MTN.

North Peak
4,293 ft.

Little Haystack
4,840 ft.

South Peak
4,358 ft.

The Basin

Mt. Liberty
4,459 ft.

N

The Flume

Flume Brook

Mt. Flume
4,328 ft.

0   1   2

MILES

EXIT 1
Franconia
Notch Pkwy

93

Flume Visitor
Center

3

TO
LINCOLN

14

2.0	Pass more restrooms on the right as you pass the upper Basin parking area.
2.4	Cross a bridge.
2.7	Cross a bridge.
3.2	Cross a bridge.
3.5	Enter the parking area of Lafayette Place Campground. Ride through the parking lot past the Lonesome Lake Trailhead on the left and the information center (a brown log cabin) farther on the right. Look for the bike-route sign marking the trail as it continues out the north end of the parking lot.
3.6	Admire the fine view of Cannon Cliff towering above as you cross a small bridge and then the Pemi Trail.
4.9	Cross a bridge and continue into the Profile Lake parking area. Profile Lake is the headwaters of the Pemigewasset River and is well known for its brook trout (fly fishing only). This is a great spot to stop and look for climbers ascending the many routes on the massive granite faces of Cannon Cliff. Exit the north end of the parking lot and continue through a tunnel under the parkway.
5.2	Cross a small bridge and note the fine view of Profile Lake, often called the "Old Man's Washbowl," because it lies directly below the Old Man of the Mountain's great stone profile.
5.4	Pass into the Old Man viewing area, where you get excellent views of the New Hampshire state icon. The Old Man of the Mountain is a stone profile hovering 1,200 feet above Profile Lake to the west. Follow the bike-route sign out the north end of the parking lot.
5.7	Cross through a tunnel under the parkway. The ride continues north (turn right), but you may wish to go south (left), first taking time to see the Profile Lake Interpretive Center and further views of the Old Man and Profile Lake.
5.8	Stay right, crossing through the parking lot, or follow

the trail to the left if you feel the need for gifts and ice cream. Regain the trail at the upper (north) end past a "Closed to Unauthorized Vehicles" sign.

6.0   At a stop sign, cross the road to the Cannon Mountain Aerial Tramway and the New England Ski Museum. Both of these are worth a look.

6.3   Stay right at the trail junction, continuing around Echo Lake's east side. After thorough testing I couldn't find an echo, but try your luck.

6.9   At a fork with a trail leaving to the left and a tunnel straight ahead, turn around and return via the same route.

Variation 1: From the top of the ride, at 6.9 miles, continue through the tunnel on a paved trail descending the north side of Franconia Notch for 2.2 miles to the Skookumchuck Trailhead.

Variation 2: From the top of the ride, at 6.9 miles, follow the path to the left up to New Hampshire 18. Turn left; in about 50 yards, the Echo Lake parking area gives access to lake swimming, picnic areas, hiking, and restrooms.

Variation 3: This route can be ridden one way in reverse by leaving a vehicle at the Flume Gorge parking area and driving a second vehicle to Echo Lake. Follow Franconia Notch State Parkway north (Interstate 93) to exit 3 (Echo Lake, Peabody Slopes). Turn left and cross over the parkway on New Hampshire 18 north for 0.7 mile and park on the right at the hiker parking area opposite Cannon Mountain Ski Area. Begin the ride by returning down New Hampshire 18 (south) for 0.6 mile past the Echo Lake parking area. Descend the paved trail on the right by the guardrail. The ride begins in reverse, from mile 6.9 (see description), as you join the main bike path.

Lincoln Woods Trail (The Wilderness Trail)

Location: 5 miles east of Interstate 93, exit 32, just off Kancamagus Highway (New Hampshire 112) in White Mountain National Forest.

Distance: 6.4-mile loop.

Time: 50 minutes to 1.5 hours.

Tread: 2.9 miles on jeep trail; 0.6 mile on singletrack; 2.9 miles on doubletrack (old logging railroad bed).

Aerobic level: Easy.

Technical difficulty: 2 on jeep trail and doubletrack; 3 on singletrack.

Highlights: Riding through mixed forest, you get views of the East Branch of the Pemigewasset River and the White Mountains. The return side of this loop follows a section of the old East Branch and Lincoln logging railroad bed. An excellent waterfall and swimming hole are accessible via a short side trip.

Hazards: Don't cross the stream between Pemi East Road and the Lincoln Woods Trail unless water levels are low enough to be safe. The crossing requires balance for stepping across stones while

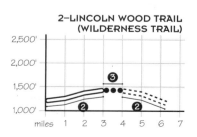

2–LINCOLN WOOD TRAIL (WILDERNESS TRAIL)

carrying a bike. Bikes must be carried up a steep bank after crossing the stream.

Land status: White Mountain National Forest.

Maps: WMNF Mountain Bike Map; AMC Map 5 Franconia; USDA Forest Service WMNF "Hiking Lincoln Woods Trail" brochure; USGS Mount Osceola Quadrangle.

Access: From Interstate 93, take exit 32. Go east on Kancamagus Highway (New Hampshire 112) for 5 miles to the Lincoln Woods Trail parking lot located on the north (left) side of the highway; there is parking for 160 cars. The trail leaves from the north end of the parking lot, past the information and ranger station.

The ride

- **0.0** The trail leaves the north side of the parking lot past the information center. Follow the service-road sign, staying east of the river.
- **0.2** Singletrack spur trail veers to right (0.1 mile to grassy clearing and viewpoint; go snap some photos and return to main trail); continue north.
- **0.6** Short, moderate rise in trail followed by short descent.
- **1.1** Spur trail on left goes to clearing. Continue straight.
- **2.2** Outhouse on left. Continue straight.
- **2.6** Scenic overlook to the west with a great view of the river and mountains.
- **2.9** Boundary gate for WMNF Wilderness Area; bikes not allowed beyond the gate. Follow the road to the west (left) down the hill or return from here if the river crossing is unsafe (see Variation below).
- **3.0** Stay right at the turnaround at the bottom of the hill and continue out to the river. Cross river (conditions permitting) on stones.

LINCOLN WOODS TRAIL
Ride 2

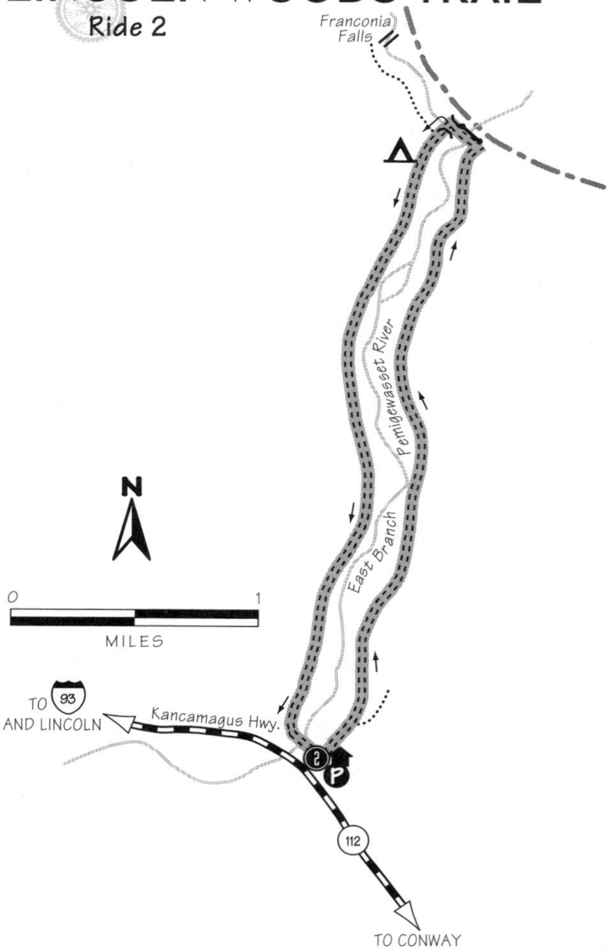

Franconia
Falls

Pemigewasset River

East Branch

N

0   1

MILES

TO 93
AND LINCOLN

Kancamagus Hwy.

P

112

TO CONWAY

19

3.2	Stay right after crossing the river; cross Franconia Brook, and join a singletrack trail up the far bank.
3.3	Climb the steep bank to gain the trail on the north side of a wooden footbridge (some may wish to ford the brook to an easier climb on the south side of the bridge). Turn left (south) on the trail and cross the bridge to a wide, old railroad bed and dark forest corridor of Lincoln Woods Trail.
3.4	Franconia Falls Trail leaves to the west (right). (There is an outhouse on Franconia Falls Trail; see Variations below for details.) Continue straight.
4.1	Continue past Franconia Brook Campsite.
4.3	Black Pond Trail leaves to the west (right); continue straight.
5.0	After a long straight stretch, cross Birch Island Brook on a small wooden bridge.
5.1	Black Pond Trail leaves to the west (right); continue straight.
5.2	River comes close to trail, providing a nice view of Mount Bond.
5.4	Site of Old Logging Camp 8.
5.6	Osceo Trail leaves to west (right); continue straight.
6.2	Trail crosses small wooden bridge; continue straight.
6.4	Turn left and cross suspension bridge back to parking lot.

Variation 1: If you do not feel up to carrying your bike or are not confident about making the river crossing, turn around at the wilderness area boundary gate and return on the same trail.

Variation 2: The 0.3-mile trail out to Franconia Falls is a very difficult ride with lots of roots, ruts, and rocks. It can be easily hiked, however, and is well worth the effort.

Variation 3: The main loop can be ridden in reverse, but the old railroad bed has lots of railroad ties still in place and is more easily navigated going downhill.

Kancamagus Race Course

Location: 1.7 miles east of Interstate 93, exit 32, in Lincoln.

Distance: 8.8-mile loop.

Time: 1 to 2 hours.

Tread: 1.2 miles on jeep trail; 0.2 mile on paved road; 7.4 miles on singletrack.

Aerobic level: Moderate.

Technical difficulty: 2 on jeep trail; 1 on paved road; 2 to 3, 4 on singletrack.

Highlights: This route is used as a mountain-bike race course and offers fast, fun, singletrack riding in a loop. There are three crossover trails that can be used to vary the length of the ride.

Land status: White Mountain National Forest; private; town.

Maps: USGS Lincoln Quadrangle (but the route is not shown on any map).

Access: From Interstate 93, exit 32, go east at the stoplight at the bottom of the ramp on New Hampshire 112 (Lincoln's Main

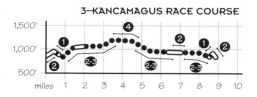

Street and Kancamagus Highway). Go 1.4 miles, past a stop-light and two blinking lights. Turn left as you leave town at a sign for Forest Ridge Townhomes. Go 0.3 mile to the Kancamagus Recreation Area, a small ski area with a basketball court, on the right. Turn into the parking lot and pick a spot. The trail leaves from the parking lot; ride west between the buildings, on gravel, across the base of the ski slope.

The ride

0.0   From the parking lot, ride west on gravel between the buildings, onto the grass, and to the right of the shed before the baseball field. Head for the leftmost ski trail and begin a strenuous climb to its top. Level 2.

0.2   At the top of the ski slope, by the base of a water tank, turn left onto a gravel road and descend.

0.3   Join a paved road, staying right. Level 1.

0.4   Turn right into an area that usually has stacks of fire-wood, as the paved road turns left. Look for a singletrack climbing into the woods. Level 2 to 3.

0.5   The trail bends left and descends to an intermittent stream. Cross the boulders and climb the far side for 50 yards, staying right as you join, and continue climbing on a more worn singletrack.

0.6   Stay left at this Y, climbing over several water bars and through raspberries and tall brush. The right branch climbs very steeply to "First Ledge" with good views of the valley and Lincoln.

0.9   The trail levels as you cross a deep, intermittent stream and begin a gradual descent, traversing the hillside.

1.6   Pass a logging trail on the left.

1.7   Turn right on the jeep trail across a buried culvert. Follow the main, more used trail from here. Don't be confused by the many side trails and pullouts left from when this

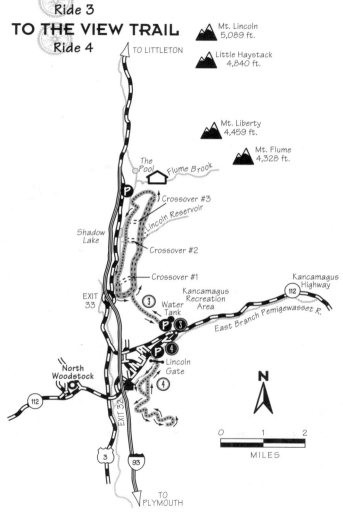

KANCAMAGUS RACE COURSE
Ride 3
TO THE VIEW TRAIL
Ride 4

Mt. Lincoln
5,089 ft.

Little Haystack
4,840 ft.

Mt. Liberty
4,459 ft.

Mt. Flume
4,328 ft.

TO LITTLETON

The Pool

Flume Brook

P

Crossover #3

Lincoln Reservoir

Shadow Lake

Crossover #2

Crossover #1

EXIT 33

③

Water Tank

Kancamagus Recreation Area

P ③

Kancamagus Highway

112

East Branch Pemigewasset R.

P ④

Lincoln Gate

④

North Woodstock

112

EXIT 32

3

93

N

0   1   2

MILES

TO PLYMOUTH

23

area was Campers World Campground. This is also the intersection you will return to from the loop portion of this ride.

1.8 Pass through a clearing with a large dirt pile on the right. Reenter the woods as the trail becomes single-track on old road.

2.0 Pass Crossover Trail #1 on the left, which may be used to shorten the loop.

2.1 Pass through a grassy clearing with rocks and ruts on the trail. As you reenter the woods, stay to the left at the Y intersection.

2.2 Stay to the left, past a trail on the right, as the trail bends left. The trail narrows slightly and becomes grassy.

2.3 After crossing a water bar, climb to a rise and begin to descend. Use caution on a washed-out culvert pipe.

2.4 The trail opens up a little.

2.6 Cross an intermittent stream as the trail bends left and descends.

2.7 At a complex trail junction, continue on worn single-track straight over a wooden bridge. Begin a long gradual climb after an intermittent stream. The trail entering from the left rear is Crossover Trail #2, and the trail to the right goes up to the Lincoln Reservoir.

2.8 Cross an intermittent stream.

3.1 Continue past Crossover Trail #3 on the left. Look for a sign on the right indicating you are continuing on the "Old Lombard Trail," a beautiful, wide, cross-country ski trail.

3.3 The trail climbs more steeply over washed-out sections.

3.8 Cross a large culvert pipe as the trail bends to the left, making a steep, more technical descent. Level 4.

3.9 Cross an intermittent stream.

4.0 Cross an intermittent stream as the trail bends slightly right, levels for a moment, and descends again through an S turn.

4.1 Cross an intermittent stream as the trail descends steeply and crosses a series of four small wooden bridges.

4.2 Continue to descend over a series of exposed granite slabs.

4.3 At the base of a granite slab, the trail bends sharply to the left; follow it down the Pemigewasset River. A cross-country ski trail on the right (posted with a sign that says, "The Flume Trail") leaves from this corner to the right. Consider carrying across logs in the trail.

4.5 Cross a wooden bridge.

4.7 Make a zigzag on washed-out trail, left then right, and cross a bridge.

4.8 Swing closer to the river as the trail improves. Level 2 to 3.

5.0 Turn left at an intersection with a trail on the right that crosses the river on a large bridge and goes to Indian Head Resort.

5.1 Notice a sign on the left for Vista Point, a look into a beaver pond. Continue past a trail a bit farther on the left.

5.3 Cross a bridge and veer away from the river.

5.4 Cross another bridge and bear right just after it onto narrower singletrack. (The trail straight ahead is the other end of Crossover Trail #3). Level 3.

5.5 Consider carrying across two consecutive streams.

5.7 Cross a very rideable stream with a sandy bottom, followed by a separate stream that is more rocky.

5.8 Turn left onto the old roadbed. Ride about 30 yards and turn right back onto singletrack. This is Crossover Trail #2.

6.2 Use caution as the trail bends sharply right and crosses a stream on a log and large rock. Ride along the river again.

6.3 The trail bends sharply left, dropping to cross the stream again. Cross and follow to the right across the hillside.

6.4 Cross two intermittent streams.

6.6 Join the jeep trail, staying right at the base of Crossover Trail #1. Level 2.

6.7 At a patch of pavement, go left, climbing sandy trail past a stone retaining wall. To the right is a bridge to U.S. Highway 3.

6.9 Follow the trail as it switches back left, climbing around two large boulders.

7.0 Follow the jeep trail left, around a manhole cover and a boulder before a trail on the right.

7.1 Turn right onto the singletrack you rode in on. You're heading home! Climb gradually, traversing the hillside. Level 2 to 3.

7.2 Pass a trail on the right.

7.8 As you pass into a raspberry patch, cross a deep, intermittent stream and begin to descend over several water bars.

8.2 Pass the turnoff for First Ledge on the left. Don't go too fast from here and miss the turn, in less than 0.1 mile onto less-worn trail and over an intermittent stream crossing. If you end up behind the condos, you've gone too far.

8.4 Turn left on the paved road, past the log area, and climb.

8.5 Stay left onto the dirt road.

8.6 At the water tank, turn right and carve a few turns as you descend the ski trail.

8.8 Back at the parking lot.

To the View Trail

[See map page 23]

Location: 0.7 mile east of Interstate 93, exit 32, in Woodstock.

Distance: 4.8-mile round trip.

Time: 1.5 to 2 hours.

Tread: 0.6 mile on paved road; 2.7 miles on jeep trail; 1.5 miles on singletrack.

Aerobic level: Easy, with a strenuous climb to the view on jeep trail.

Technical difficulty: 1 on paved road; 2 and 2+ on jeep trail; 3 on singletrack.

Highlights: A really nice ride along the river climbing steeply to "The View" of the mountains to the north and west of Lincoln.

Land status: Private and White Mountain National Forest.

Maps: USGS Lincoln Quadrangle.

Access: From Interstate 93, exit 32, go east at the stoplight at the bottom of the ramp onto New Hampshire 112 (Lincoln's Main Street and Kancamagus Highway). Go 0.7 mile, past a stoplight and two blinking lights. Just past the second blinking light, park on the

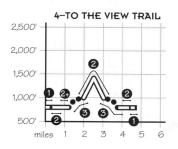

4–TO THE VIEW TRAIL

right at the Lincoln town offices (look for a blue-and-white parking sign). The ride begins from the parking lot and heads east on New Hampshire 112.

The ride

0.0 From the parking lot, ride east on New Hampshire 112 (Main Street); turn right in 50 yards at the second driveway by the Rivergreen Resort Hotel and Links Condominiums. Level 1.

0.2 Follow the paved road left.

0.3 Cross the East Branch of the Pemigewasset on a bridge with railings. Turn right at the end of the bridge on the dirt road. Stay right as you enter the parking lot, descending past a wooden gate onto a jeep trail that follows the river's edge. Look for cross-country ski trail signs and "To the View" painted on the gate. Level 2.

0.6 Pass a trail on the left as you ride into a grassy clearing. Stay right along the river on the far side of the clearing, following the sign indicating "the best direction to ski"; it's also the best direction to ride. You will return on the left-hand trail. Level 2+.

1.0 Look for a trail on the right, just before the national forest boundary marker, descending to a large rock and a good swimming hole. Past the marker, the ride climbs steeply over water bars and up a short hill.

1.4 The trail climbs left and away from the river onto more grassy trail.

1.5 As the trail switches back to the left, follow the singletrack leaving to the right and marked with a sign that says "View." Level 3.

1.6 Pass through a small grassy clearing and ride over water bars after reentering the woods.

1.8 Cross a small rocky stream in a deep bed.

1.9 Stay left at the trail junction with a wide, grassy, jeep trail. Note the "View" sign on a tree. Climb steeply through many switchbacks. Level 2.

2.5 Admire the view to the right along this flat section above an old clearcut. Mount Kinsman, Cannon with its tower, and Lafayette are all visible. The trail continues for a short distance farther without views. Most people turn around here and start the fast descent.

3.1 Turn right onto the singletrack trail. Level 3.

3.2 Cross the small rocky stream in a deep bed.

3.5 As you join the wide, grassy, ski trail, turn right, opposite the way you came, riding under abandoned powerlines; some poles remain, but there are no wires.

3.8 Pass the national forest boundary.

4.2 Rejoin the trail you rode in on, staying right at a clearing. Ride across the clearing and past a trail on the right as you enter the woods with the river on your left. Level 2.

4.5 Pass around the gate up to the parking area. Stay left onto paved road across the bridge. Level 1.

4.6 Stay right on the road.

4.8 Turn left onto New Hampshire 112, returning to the parking lot in 50 yards.

Bog Brook Eddy

Location: 0.4 mile west of Interstate 93 north, exit 33, in Lincoln.

Distance: 3.2-mile one way.

Time: 1 to 1.5 hours.

Tread: 1 mile of very rough jeep trail; 1.3 miles of ATV-width doubletrack.

Aerobic level: Moderate to strenuous.

Technical difficulty: 2 and 4+ on jeep trail, 3- on ATV-width doubletrack.

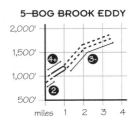

Highlights: This ride switches back and forth between smooth trail and technical rock pounding as you make a continuous ascent to Bog Brook Eddy (a widening in the brook that looks like a pond below the actual Bog Pond). However, you are rewarded for your efforts with a look at a classic blackwater mountain bog with peat- and sphagnum-moss islands. Listen for the steam engine train whistle echoing across the valley from Lincoln as you climb.

Land status: White Mountain National Forest.

Maps: WMNF Mountain Bike Map; DeLorme New Hampshire Atlas and Gazetteer, 10th edition; USGS Lincoln Quadrangle.

Access: From Interstate 93, exit 33, go north onto U.S. Highway 3. Go 0.2 mile and turn left onto Hanson Farm Road, just after the Profile Motel. In 0.1 mile, stay left going down the dead-end street. Park in the small parking lot at the end of the road on the right. The ride begins as you pass through the opening in the chain-link fence at the end of the road.

The ride

0.0 Pass through the opening in the chain-link fence at the end of the road. Ride under the northbound lane of Interstate 93 through a tunnel, staying left at the intersection on the far side. Level 2.

BOG BROOK EDDY
Ride 5
NORTH WOODSTOCK RESERVOIR LOOP
Ride 6
GORDON POND
Ride 7

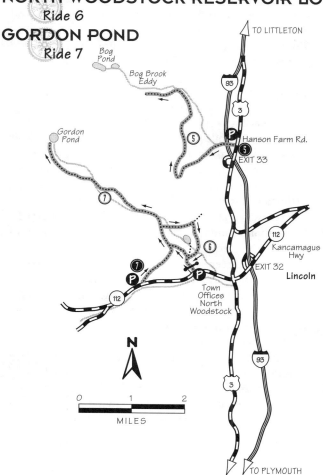

TO LITTLETON

Bog
Pond

Bog Brook
Eddy

93

3

Gordon
Pond

5

P

Hanson Farm Rd.

5

EXIT 33

7

6

112

7

P

112

Kancamagus
Hwy

EXIT 32

Lincoln

P

Town
Offices
North
Woodstock

93

3

N

0   1   2

MILES

TO PLYMOUTH

0.1   Cross a bridge and follow the trail under the south-bound lane of Interstate 93. Immediately turn left onto the narrow track and ride south along Interstate 93 for a short distance.

0.2   Follow the trail to the right as it enters the woods and opens to a jeep trail.

0.3   Continue straight through a trail junction and over a culvert pipe. The trail becomes rocky and sandy as you begin the long climb to Bog Brook Eddy.

0.6   Climb more steeply over loose boulders and sand as a snowmobile trail enters from the left. Level 4+.

0.9   Cross over logs set into the trail.

1.0   Pass a snowmobile trail on the right and continue over a deep water bar. In about 20 yards, cross a crude log bridge; be careful not to get your tires stuck between the logs of this masterpiece. The trail difficulty eases a little as it narrows to ATV-width doubletrack. Cross several technical water bars with logs in them. Level 3-.

1.3   Cross an intermittent stream on stacked logs as the trail switches back to the right and follows the hillside, alternating between smooth and rough technical trail.

2.0   Pass a snowmobile trail descending to the right.

2.5   Cross a stream on a scary-looking snowmobile bridge.

2.6   Climb through a particularly washed-out section of trail with loose sand and boulders ranging in size from marbles to truck tires.

3.0   The trail becomes grassy on a sand base. Listen for cascading water, to the right, flowing from the bog.

3.2   Get your first glimpse of Bog Brook Eddy. The trail continues along the edge of the bog, giving good views of Franconia Ridge and Mount Pemigewasset. Return via the same route.

North Woodstock Reservoir Loop

[See map page 31]

Location: 1.2 miles west of Interstate 93, exit 32, in North Woodstock.

Distance: 2.6-mile loop.

Time: 30 to 45 minutes.

Tread: 1.1 miles on ATV-width doubletrack; 1.1 miles on jeep trail; 0.2 mile on dirt road; 0.2 mile on paved road.

Aerobic level: Moderate.

Technical difficulty: 1 on paved and dirt roads; 2 on jeep trail; 3 on ATV-width doubletrack.

Highlights: A short, fairly easy loop in an area with many more trails to explore.

Land status: Private; town; White Mountain National Forest.

Maps: USGS Lincoln Quadrangle

Access: From Interstate 93, exit 32, go west at the stoplight at the bottom of the ramp onto New Hampshire 112 (Main Street). Go 1.2 miles (through the stoplight at U.S. Highway 3 at 0.7 mile) to the Woodstock police and town offices parking lot on the left. The ride begins by riding farther west on New Hampshire 112.

6–NORTH WOODSTOCK RESERVOIR LOOP

The ride

0.0 From the town offices, ride west on New Hampshire 112.

0.1 Turn right onto Clark Farm Road. Go straight past a driveway on the right at the beginning of the road.

0.2 Ride between the house and barn to the end of the road. Turn left onto sandy jeep trail and continue around the aluminum gate as you enter the woods. Level 2.

0.4 Pass the national forest property boundary through a Forest Service gate.

0.5 As the trail dips and begins to climb to the left, pass a snowmobile trail on the right. This is where you will emerge on the return.

0.8 Stay left at the Y intersection onto more rocky, less worn trail. To the right is the town watertank and reservoir pond if you wish to have a look. Level 2+.

0.9 Stay right as a trail joins from the left. The Gordon Pond Trail joins here (Ride 7).

1.0 Cross two consecutive bridges and a water bar. In 20 yards, by a blue blaze on a tree, turn right on Murry's Trail, an ATV-width doubletrack trail on the right. Level 3.

1.1 Cross wide, boulder-strewn Gordon Pond Brook. Rejoin the trail slightly downstream on the opposite side. The trail climbs sharply until you gain old logging railway bed that descends gradually. Use caution crossing the brook in high water.

1.2 Cross a snowmobile bridge.

1.4 Cross an intermittent stream.

1.5 Turn right onto a snowmobile trail after several whoop-de-doos and a short rise that brings you to wider trail. The route finding can be somewhat difficult in the beginning, but, generally, you descend staying right.

1.6	The trail improves and route finding is easier.
1.9	Turn right at the base of the descent on a trail that crosses a large wooden snowmobile bridge with railings. Watch for a "Trail Junction" sign on the descent preceding this turn.
2.0	Pass through an opening in the woods on grassy trail and stay right at a trail junction on the far side before reentering the woods.
2.1	Turn left onto the jeep trail that you rode in on. Level 2.
2.2	Pass through the Forest Service gate and out of the national forest.
2.4	Pass around the aluminum gate and turn right around the barn onto Clark Farm Road. Level 1.
2.5	Turn east (left) onto New Hampshire 112.
2.6	Turn right into the town offices parking lot.

Variation: Join this ride with Gordon Pond Trail (Ride 7).

Gordon Pond Trail
[See map page 31]

Location: 2.5 miles west of Interstate 93, exit 32, in North Woodstock.

Distance: 4.7-mile one way.

Time: 2 to 3 hours.

Tread: 0.6 mile on jeep trail; 2.7 miles on ATV-width doubletrack; 1.3 miles on singletrack.

Aerobic level: Easy for the first 1.7 miles, then climbs strenuously.

Technical difficulty: 2, 2+, and 4 on jeep trail; 2+ to 4 on ATV-width doubletrack; 3-4 on singletrack.

Highlights: Fun riding on easy trail following mostly old railroad bed for the first 1.7 miles. The trail becomes more of a challenge as it climbs, long and hard, up to the pond.

Land status: White Mountain National Forest; private land.

Maps: WMNF Mountain Bike Map; DeLorme New Hampshire Atlas and Gazetteer, 10th edition; USGS Lincoln and Mount Moosilauke quadrangles.

Access: From Interstate 93, exit 32, go west at the stoplight (at the bottom of the ramp) on New Hampshire 112 (Main Street). Go 2.4 miles through the traffic light in the village of Woodstock (0.6 mile) and turn right onto Mountain Side Road opposite Agassiz Basin and Govoni's Restaurant; look for the "Gordon Pond Trailhead" sign. Go less than 0.1 mile past houses, staying left onto the dirt road. Park at one of the pullouts on the left or right. The ride begins 50 yards farther up the road at a four-way intersection.

The ride

0.0 About 50 yards farther up the road, you'll come to an unmarked intersection with a "No Trespassing" sign on the trail straight ahead. Turn to the right, onto the jeep trail, and then follow the old railroad grade past an arrow on a tree to the right. Level 2.

0.2   Pass a log landing on the left as the trail narrows to ATV-width doubletrack.

0.5   Follow the trail arrow to the left and ride up wide, grassy trail under the powerlines. Level 3.

0.7   Turn right following the trail arrow and enter the woods. The trail descends.

0.9   Turn left at the arrow, regaining old railroad bed. Level 2+.

1.2   Stay left as you join a logging road, then continue left on a jeep trail with loose sand and rock.

1.3   Cross two consecutive bridges and a snowmobile trail on the right. The North Woodstock Reservoir Loop (Ride 6) follows this trail to the right.

1.6   The trail becomes washed out with many large, loose rocks. Level 4.

1.7   Stay to the left at a trail junction (do not cross the creek). Pass under the powerlines on ATV-width doubletrack, which becomes rocky and root infested as you gradually climb.

2.0   Just after joining the brook, cross it on the right by descending a steep bank and carrying over large boulders.

2.2   As the trail bends to the right, begin climbing more steeply. Level 4.

2.7   Cross a snowmobile bridge and ascend on the far side.

2.8   Cross an intermittent stream and climb, traversing the hillside.

3.4   Cross a bridge spanning high over a swath of water-smoothed granite rubble descending steeply through the forest. The trail begins a long, steep ascent on narrow singletrack trail traversing the seemingly endless hillside. Level 3 to 4.

3.6   Ascend a section of ledge that all but superhumans will probably have to carry across.

3.8   Use extreme caution as you cross the brook on slippery, mossy ledge high atop a waterfall.

3.9 Cross back over the brook on mossy rocks and carry through a muddy, rutted section of trail; the trail is often very muddy from here; look for auxiliary trails on the sides. Level 4.

4.5 Carry around a very swampy section of trail.

4.6 Cross a brook over rocks.

4.7 Pass through a campsite before coming to the pond's edge.

Variation: Join this ride with North Woodstock Reservoir Loop (Ride 6).

Cilley Mountain Loop

Location: 2.2 miles west of Interstate 93, exit 30, in Woodstock.

Distance: 10.7-mile loop.

Time: 3 to 6 hours.

Tread: 0.8 mile on paved road; 1.1 miles on dirt road; 0.6 mile on jeep trail; 0.9 mile on ATV-width doubletrack; 4.7 miles on ATV-width singletrack; 2.6 miles on singletrack.

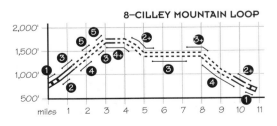

Aerobic level: Strenuous climb for the first 2.3 miles, then mostly level or descending.

Technical difficulty: 1 on paved road; 1 and 2 on dirt road; 2+ on jeep trail; 2+, 3, 4, and 5 on ATV-width doubletrack; 3 on ATV-width singletrack; 3+ and 4 on singletrack.

Highlights: This trail offers a great mix of tread and technical difficulties on a long loop ride. It also has historical significance. The start takes you through the village of Peeling, Woodstock's original settlement, which was abandoned about the time of the Civil War.

Land status: White Mountain National Forest; private lands; town roads.

Maps: WMNF Mountain Bike Map; DeLorme New Hampshire Atlas and Gazetteer, 10th edition; AMC Map 4 Chocorua-Waterville; USGS Woodstock and Lincoln quadrangles.

Access: From Interstate 93, exit 30, go north on U.S. Highway 3 for 2.2 miles. Turn left into the parking lot of Woodstock Town Hall. The ride begins by heading north on U.S. Highway 3 from the parking lot.

The ride

0.0 Ride north on U.S. Highway 3 from Woodstock Town Hall.

0.5 Turn left onto Mount Cilley Road, opposite the Original Design (OD) Silk Screen Company. Begin the agonizing climb on loose sand and gravel. Level 2.

0.9 As the gravel-surfaced road appears to end at a house, veer left onto an old roadbed now covered with grass and ferns. Continue climbing into the woods on ATV-width doubletrack. Level 3.

1.3 Cross a small wooden bridge.

1.5 Cross another small wooden bridge and climb through

CILLEY MOUNTAIN LOOP
Ride 8

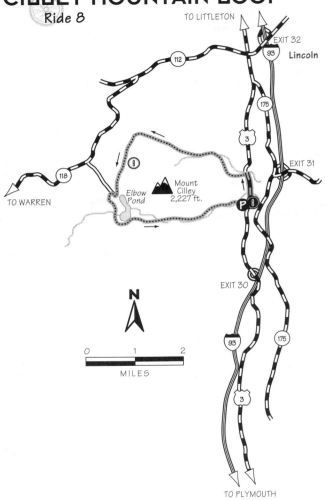

TO LITTLETON

EXIT 32

93 Lincoln

112

175

3

8

EXIT 31

Mount
Cilley
2,227 ft.

Elbow
Pond

118

TO WARREN

P 8

EXIT 30

N

93

175

0   1   2

MILES

3

TO PLYMOUTH

several technical sections as the climb resumes on the far side. The trail narrows to ATV-width singletrack, becoming more overgrown. Level 4.

2.1 Cross an intermittent stream, continuing to climb sharply over trenched trail with large, loose rocks, logs, and sand. Level 5.

2.3 As the trail levels and eases in difficulty, pause at a green trail sign on the right that indicates you are on the Mount Cilley Trail. If you look down, you will realize that this was once the village street of Peeling; note the overgrown granite blocks that were once a culvert under the street. About 20 yards to the right is an overgrown building foundation. Continue after you've had a look. Level 3.

2.4 Pass over another old culvert on this storybook ride as you continue through enchanted forest on mossy, leafy trail.

2.6 Cross another stone culvert.

2.7 Descend on narrow, rocky, and root-infested trail. Level 5.

2.9 Finish the gnarly descent over a snowmobile bridge. Level 4-.

3.1 Make a stream crossing on slick moss-covered rocks.

3.3 Cross a culvert, beautifully covered with moss, as a stone wall parallels the trail on the right. This area may once have been the town square; use your imagination and look for additional foundations.

3.4 Cross another stone culvert before riding onto a grassy, fern-lined section of trail surrounded by young trees.

4.0 Cross another stone culvert.

4.3 Stay left at a Y, and continue descending to a Forest Service road. Turn right and descend straight past another road entering from the left (jeep trail). Level 2+.

4.7 Pass through a log landing.

4.9 Pass around several large boulders into a parking area at the end of Forest Service Road 156 (dirt road). There is an excellent view of the north opening of Elbow Pond if you ride 0.3 mile to the left along the pond's east shore (return to this point to continue with the ride looping around the west shore). Continue the ride by turning northwest (right) and descending Forest Service Road 156. Pass a trail blocked by a boulder about 50 yards down the road on the left.

5.3 Turn left onto ATV-width singletrack 30 yards past a pullout on the left (Forest Service Road 156 continues out to New Hampshire 118). This trail cruises on the soft, level ground of an old railroad bed through a tunnel of trees. This section of trail can get very muddy. Level 3.

6.3 Ride past a trail joining from the right.

6.9 Stay right, and right again at an X intersection. In 100 yards, follow a smaller trail to the left to avoid a dropoff where a railroad bridge once crossed a brook.

7.0 Cross the sandy-bottomed brook and stay right to regain the railroad bed. Turn left on the railroad bed, soon crossing an intermittent stream over logs and stones.

7.2 Cross two intermittent streams. In 25 yards, you'll come to a trail on the left that looks like the main trail and leads to a campsite at the edge of Elbow Pond's south opening. There is a fine view of the pond from the campsite, with Mount Cilley centered to the east between the notch you came through to the north and the notch you will descend through to the south. Check out the old truck carcass near the campsite. Continue the ride on overgrown singletrack past a rusty steel pipe driven into the ground at this intersection. The trail follows around the pond. Level 3+.

7.5 Drop down into a swampy area as the trail heads away from the pond.

7.6 Pass a trail leading to the pond's edge on the left.

7.8	Work your way through a muddy, grassy clearing, with a trail entering from the left rear.
7.9	Cross over a rocky stream.
8.1	The trail bends right and follows down the bank of Glover Brook.
8.2	Cross to the other side of Glover Brook and continue to descend on narrow trail with increased obstacles, some requiring carries. Level 4.
8.7	Traverse three consecutive streambeds.
8.8	Pass a national forest boundary marker as you descend through very rideable rock problems.
9.1	Use caution as you make a fast, steep descent to a water bar (essentially, it's all downhill from here).
9.6	Make a stream crossing over large, loose rocks.
9.8	At an intermittent stream, look for the narrower singletrack trail as it climbs up to the left, away from the obvious roadbed at the edge of a deep granite canyon. The singletrack soon opens to ATV-width doubletrack as it follows a terrace above the canyon on wide, smooth trail. Level 2+.
10.1	Cross Glover Brook at a very pretty spot where stonework from an old bridge remains. Step easily across the brook on large boulders. Stay right on the far bank, going left as you regain the old roadbed (or see Variation below). Ride 100 yards and turn left at a granite post with "Donahue" carved into it, opposite a sand and gravel pit. Descend on Potato Hill Road (dirt).
10.4	Go north (left) on U.S. Highway 3.
10.7	Pass the graveyard and finish at Woodstock Town Hall.

Variation:

10.1 Turn left on the far bank and look for a narrow single-track. The singletrack is often hard to follow, but it offers fun riding all the way down the edge of Glover Brook to U.S. Highway 3. Follow the path of least resistance past an abundance of fine swimming holes. Level 5.

10.6 Cross over Old U.S. Highway 3, which looks like a highway out of a Mad Max movie, and descend to present-day U.S. Highway 3. Go south (right) and ride a short distance to Woodstock Town Hall on the right.

10.7 End of ride.

Rumney

Ellsworth Pond

(Forest Service Road 348 to Forest Service Road 112)

Location: 5.7 miles west of Interstate 93, exit 28, in Ellsworth.

Distance: 6.4-mile loop.

Time: 40 minutes to 2 hours.

Tread: 2.7 miles on dirt road; 2.7 miles on jeep trail; 0.6 mile on ATV-width singletrack; 0.4 mile on paved road.

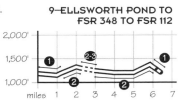

9—ELLSWORTH POND TO FSR 348 TO FSR 112

44

Aerobic level: Moderate.

Technical difficulty: 2 on jeep trail; 1 and 2 on dirt; 1 on paved road; 3 on ATV-width singletrack.

Highlights: There is a screaming downhill near the end of the ride. This trail makes a good loop that can be added to the West Branch Brook ride (Ride 13).

Hazards: Three carries are required across streams or on logs. Some traffic may be encountered on Ellsworth–Stinson Lake Road.

Land status: White Mountain National Forest and public roadways.

Maps: WMNF Mountain Bike Map; USGS Mount Kineo, Woodstock, Rumney, and Plymouth quadrangles.

Access: From Interstate 93, exit 28, turn west on New Hampshire 49, going under the overpass. At 0.1 mile, turn south (left) on U.S. Highway 3 and then immediately right onto Dan Web Road, following signs for Stinson Lake and Ellsworth. At the top of the rise, turn right onto Ellsworth Hill Road. Go 4.5 miles and turn right onto Ellsworth Village Road (gravel). Park at the Town Hall and Old Schoolhouse, opposite Saint John of the Mountains Chapel.

The ride

- **0.0** Leave the parking area and ride north on Ellsworth Village Road (dirt), through Ellsworth Village, and descend the hill. Level 1.
- **0.1** At the bottom of the hill, stay left on the main road at the intersection. The road to the right connects to the West Branch Brook ride (Ride 13).
- **0.7** The road bends right and is lined with guardrails as it crosses a stream. You get a limited view of Ellsworth Lake before the road begins to descend.

ELLSWORTH POND TO
FSR 348 TO FSR 112
Ride 9
STINSON LAKE (FSR 113 TO FSR 215)
Ride 10
THREE PONDS
Ride 11

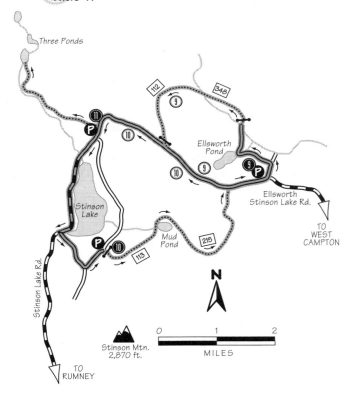

1.3	Turn left onto Forest Service Road 348 (jeep trail) just before the road ends. Level 2.
1.4	Go around the steel gate and continue straight, passing a snowmobile trail on the left.
1.7	Continue past a clearing on the left.
2.2	Cross through a clearing and turn left on the descending snowmobile trail.
2.3	Dismount and cross the West Branch Brook headwaters (future bridge site) and continue on ATV-width singletrack on the opposite side. Level 2 to 3.
2.4	Continue straight on the more used trail, past a spur trail on the left, signposted for Ellsworth Pond.
2.5	Begin a moderate uphill climb.
2.7	Trail descends.
2.9	Stay left at the Y intersection and descend steeply to a small clearing.
3.0	Turn right and cross a stream on a log skidder bridge. You are now on Forest Service Road 112 (jeep trail). Level 2
3.6	Road begins a gradual descent.
3.9	Cross a stream. There is no bridge here, but you can cross on a fallen log to the right. Continue up the road as it climbs over several water bars.
4.0	Go around the Forest Service gate, turn left, and begin a short, gradual climb on Ellsworth–Stinson Lake Road (dirt); watch for traffic. Level 2.
4.3	Enjoy a coast down the hill.
4.5	Continue past Forest Service Road 446 on the right.
4.9	Begin climbing again.
5.6	Continue climbing past Forest Service Road 215 on the right. (Stinson Lake, Ride 10, enters here.)
5.8	Crest the hill by a small cottage on the left and an orchard on the right. Begin a well-earned descent.
6.0	Road becomes paved. Level 1.

6.4 Turn left onto Ellsworth Village Road and return to your starting point.

Variation: This ride can easily be extended into a larger loop by combining it with the Stinson Lake ride (Ride 10) and the West Branch Brook ride (Ride 13).

Stinson Lake
(Forest Service Road 113 to Forest Service Road 215)

[See map page 46]

Location: 13.5 miles northwest of Interstate 93, exit 26, beginning in Rumney.

Distance: 10.7-mile loop.

Time: 1.5 to 2.5 hours.

Tread: 2.6 miles on dirt road; 1.6 miles on singletrack; 1.8 miles on paved road; 4.3 miles on gravel road.

Aerobic level: Moderate.

Technical level: 1 and 2 on dirt road and jeep trail; 3+ on ATV-width singletrack.

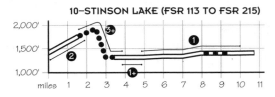

Highlights: Great views of Mead Pond and Stinson Lake. A fantastic descent at mile 2.5.

Land status: White Mountain National Forest; public roads.

Maps: WMNF Mountain Bike Map; USGS Rumney, Plymouth, and Mount Kineo quadrangles.

Access: From Interstate 93, exit 26, go west on New Hampshire 25 (Tenney Mountain Highway) for 4.0 miles to the rotary. Take the first right, following New Hampshire 25 for 3.4 miles to the second blinking yellow light. Turn right onto Stinson Lake Road (Main Street). Follow it 5.1 miles, across the Baker River, through Rumney's town center, to just before Stinson Lake. Turn right on Cross Road, by a green sign for Hawthorn Village, and go 0.5 mile (stay right at the Y intersection at 0.3 mile where the pavement ends). Turn left on Doe Town Road and go 0.3 mile. Park on the road by the entrance to Forest Service Road 113 (blocked by a green gate). The ride begins at this gate.

The ride

0.0 Follow the Forest Service road past the Forest Service gate and begin a moderately steep climb on a sandy surface, which soon becomes grassy jeep trail. Level 2.

0.4 The trail bends to the left, still climbing, past a snowmobile trail on the right.

0.5 The climb eases.

0.6 Pass a small clearing and follow the trail as it bends left, descending slightly.

1.2 Cross a washed-out culvert pipe.

1.3 Bear left at an intersection, descending slightly. The trail to the right rapidly deteriorates. Just down from the intersection is a short trail that leads out to Mead Pond and is well worth the side trip.

1.4 The trail bends to the right at the bottom of the hill and crosses a small wooden bridge. To the right is a view of the pond.

1.6 Bear right onto the narrowing trail at the intersection where a snowmobile trail enters from the left and a clearing lies straight ahead. Climb slightly on single-track as you traverse along the north side of Mead Pond.

1.7 The trail becomes more technical as you climb away from good views of the pond.

1.8 The trail crests and descends slightly.

1.9 Pick your way through rocks and ruts. Cross a small stream and bear right at an intersection, following the more used-looking trail. Level 3+.

2.0 Descend to a small clearing and, on the other side, drop down into a boggy section bridged with logs.

2.1 Begin a strenuous 0.4-mile climb, maneuvering through some rocky sections.

2.5 Top out and begin a fantastic descent, racing down the smooth trail over downed logs, maneuvering through rocks, and finishing with a steep drop at the end. Now wasn't that climb worth it? Continue as the trail follows a creek on the right.

3.0 Cross a stream.

3.2 Cross a really scary old bridge and climb a short rise to Forest Service Road 215. Turn left and follow the ATV-width singletrack across a bridge.

3.4 Cross a bridge.

3.5 Cross an old streambed.

3.6 Pop over a water bar, drop down into a clearing, and cross a bridge on the far side.

3.7 Enter a clearing and descend, following the much-improved dirt road. Level 1+.

3.8 Cross a bridge and continue left past an intersection, staying with the main road.

4.1 Pass a small clearing on the left.

4.7 Pass the Forest Service gate to the right and turn left onto descending Ellsworth–Stinson Lake Road (dirt). Level 1.

5.4 Reach the bottom of a good downhill run and start going up again.

5.8 Pass Forest Service Road 446 on the left.

6.2 Pass Forest Service Road 112 on the right (Ellsworth Pond, Ride 9, enters here).

6.4 Cross a bridge.

7.3 Cross over a bridge with a beautiful waterfall flowing under it from the right.

7.6 Begin a climb past the Three Ponds Trailhead (Ride 11) on the right.

8.1 Continue straight through an intersection onto the pavement and ride around the front of Stinson Lake.

9.6 Turn left onto Cross Road and climb, continuing around the lake.

9.9 Stay right at the intersection, following Cross Road (now a gravel surface).

10.4 Cross Road ends. Turn left onto Doe Town Road.

10.7 Find your vehicle where you left it.

Variation: The ride can be shortened slightly by turning left on Doe Town Road (Stinson Lake Back Road), 0.1 mile past the Three Ponds Trailhead on Ellsworth–Stinson Lake Road. Look for the 30 mph speed-limit sign. Follow this road directly back to the start of the ride, although you miss views of Stinson Lake. This loop can also be joined with the Ellsworth Pond ride (Ride 9).

Three Ponds

[See map page 46]

Location: 14.4 miles northwest ofInterstate 93, exit 26, in Ellsworth.

Distance: 2.3-mile one way.

Time: 25 minutes to 1 hour.

Tread: 1.3 miles on ATV-width single and doubletrack; 1 mile on singletrack.

Aerobic level: Moderate.

11–THREE PONDS

Technical difficulty: 2+ on ATV-width single and doubletrack; 4 on singletrack.

Highlights: Beautiful lake views and fast, technical downhill runs make the moderate climb worthwhile. The open-face shelter overlooking the lake provides great overnight potential for this ride.

Hazards: Several stream crossings that require carries could be hazardous in high water. One carry is required on a narrow log bridge high over the brook.

Land status: White Mountain National Forest.

Maps: WMNF Mountain Bike Map; AMC Map 4 Chocorua-Waterville; USGS Mount Kineo Quadrangle.

Access: From Interstate 93, exit 26, go west on New Hampshire 25 (Tenney Mountain Highway) for 4 miles to the rotary. Take the first right, following New Hampshire 25 for 3.4 miles to the second blinking yellow light. Turn right onto Stinson Lake Road (Main Street). Follow it 7 miles, across the Baker River, through Rumney's town center, past Stinson Lake, and across the Ellsworth town line (at 6.5 miles, where the road turns to dirt) to the Three Ponds, Carr Mountain, and Mount Kineo Trailhead parking area on the left. The trail begins at the northwest corner of the lot opposite where you enter.

The ride

0.0   Enter the woods and immediately cross a marshy area on split-log bridges. Ride up the moderate grade on ATV-width trail. Level 2+.

0.1   Continue climbing past the Mount Kineo Trail on the right for 30 yards before reaching a very technical climb (for you trials junkies).

0.4   Make a rocky stream crossing before the trail becomes singletrack, and gets muddy and more technical. Level 4. Continue following yellow blazes past the Carr Mountain Trail, which soon leaves to the left.

0.6   Cross several more split-log bridges over boggy areas.

0.9   Make a difficult small-stream crossing.

1.0   Carry across Sucker Brook on a narrow split-log bridge with one handrail. Turn right immediately on the far side, following the Three Ponds Trail sign. The ATV-width trail follows an old logging road along Sucker Brook.

1.3   Follow the yellow blazes to the right on a challenging new singletrack trail section.

1.5   Stay right as you regain the old logging road.

1.6   Diverge left to cross a stream on a large wooden bridge. If you're hot and in need of cooling off, plow straight ahead through the stream.

1.7   If you didn't get cool on that last crossing, you get another chance here. Use caution in high water and cross Sucker Brook.

1.9 Ride the rocks on a washout, which gradually climbs.

2.0 Again, use caution crossing the brook in high water. Cross the brook, ride a ditch filled with grapefruit-sized rocks, and recross the brook. The second crossing can be made by stepping from boulder to boulder.

2.1 Just as you think the trail is getting easier, follow the diversion of a new singletrack trail to the right for 0.2 mile. Level 4.

2.3 Regain the muddy logging road to the right at the south end of the first pond; follow it for several hundred feet to a Y. The left-hand option continues around the east side of the pond and becomes more difficult. The right-hand option ascends several more hundred feet to the Three Ponds Shelter. Return via the same route.

East Rumney–Campton Bog Road

Location: 3.0 miles west of Interstate 93, exit 26, in Plymouth.

Distance: 18.3-mile loop.

Time: 3.5 to 4 hours.

Tread: 11.6 miles on paved road; 6.7 miles on dirt road.

Aerobic level: Mostly easy with a long, moderate climb with several steep sections.

EAST RUMNEY–CAMPTON BOG ROAD
Ride 12

PLYMOUTH-RUMNEY RR GRADE
Ride 39

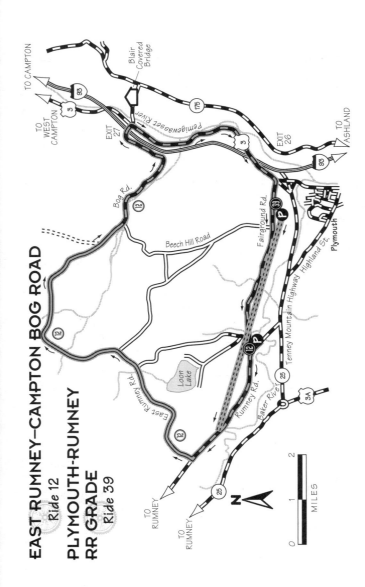

TO CAMPTON

Blair Covered Bridge

93

3

TO WEST CAMPTON

EXIT 27

Pemigewasset River

175

93

TO ASHLAND

3

EXIT 26

Bog Rd.

12

39

P

Fairground Rd.

Beech Hill Road

Plymouth

Tenney Mountain Highway Highland St.

12

12

P

Loon Lake

East Rumney Rd.

25

Rumney Rd.

Baker River

12

3A

TO RUMNEY

25

TO RUMNEY

N

0   1   2
MILES

Technical difficulty: 1 on paved roads; 2 on dirt roads.

Highlights: A technically easy loop on roads through the countryside, past farms, fields, and stone walls. Check out Blair Covered Bridge and a great swimming hole at Livermore Falls.

Hazards: Watch for traffic on U.S. Highway 3, particularly at two blind corners.

Land status: Town roads.

Maps: WMNF Mountain Bike Map; DeLorme New Hampshire Atlas and Gazetteer, 10th edition; USGS Rumney and Plymouth quadrangles.

Access: From Interstate 93, exit 26, go west on New Hampshire 25 (Tenney Mountain Highway) for 2.4 miles. Turn right onto Smith Bridge Road and go 0.6 mile, crossing the bridge, and park on the right. The ride begins by continuing west on Smith Bridge Road.

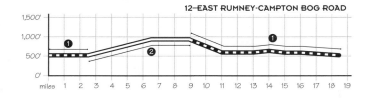

The ride

0.0   Ride west (right out of the parking area) on Smith Bridge Road.

0.1   Stay left at the Y intersection onto Quincy Road.

0.7   Pass Plymouth Municipal Airport on the left.

1.2   Cross the town line into Rumney.

1.6   Cross an old railroad grade, the end of the Plymouth-Rumney RR Grade (Ride 39).

2.4   Turn right onto East Rumney Road. Begin a long series

on this dirt road of moderate to strenuous climbs. Level 2.

5.8   Pull up over a particularly steep rise and catch a breather as you coast downhill past a small graveyard on the right. Get right back into the climbing.

6.6   Pass between two guardrails as the road bends sharply to the right and descends.

7.1   Tackle another sharp climb.

8.0   Pass a farm field lined with sugar maples on the right.

8.5   Ride past another field to the right with a fine view of the Baker River Valley.

8.7   Pass Chandler Hill Road (Ride 15) and a sugar shack on the left.

9.1   The road becomes paved. Level 1.

9.2   Pass along the edge of Rowbartwood Pond and Marsh.

9.3   Beech Hill Road leaves on the right (see Variation below).

10.9   Follow the road as it bends sharply to the left and parallels Interstate 93.

11.6   Bend sharply to the right and pass under Interstate 93.

11.8   At the stop sign and blinking light, use extreme caution as you turn south (right) onto U.S. Highway 3. This is a very busy road with some blind corners. If you like, make a side trip 100 yards across U.S. Highway 3 to Blair Covered Bridge.

13.0   Use caution at this blind bend in the road.

13.6   Watch out on this bend as well.

14.1   Cross the town line into Plymouth.

14.4   Cross under Interstate 93.

14.8   Pass the Plymouth police station on the right.

15.0   Turn right onto Fairgrounds Road opposite McDonald's.

15.8   Pass Beach Hill Road on the right and Cooksville Road, the beginning of the Plymouth-Rumney RR Grade (Ride 39), on the left. (See Variations below.)

16.3   Pass the Plymouth Fairgrounds on the right.

17.6   Cross the Plymouth-Rumney RR Grade (Ride 39).

18.1 Stay left at the Y intersection onto Smith Bridge Road.
18.3 End of the ride.

Variation: You can make the loop shorter and avoid the traffic on U.S. Highway 3 by turning right, at 9.3 miles, on Beech Hill Road, regaining the ride at 15.8 miles on Fairgrounds Road. The bad news is you gain an extra hill climb. The good news is it's followed by a descent. From this point you can avoid riding some of Fairgrounds Road by crossing onto Cooksville Road and riding the Plymouth-Rumney RR Grade (Ride 39).

Campton

West Branch Brook

(Forest Service Road 378)

Location: 0.8 mile west of Interstate 93, exit 29, in the towns of Campton, Thornton, and Ellsworth.

Distance: 4.4-mile one way.

Time: 50 minutes to 1.5 hours.

Tread: 2.7 miles on jeep trail; 1.5 miles on ATV-width singletrack; 0.2 mile on dirt road.

Aerobic level: Moderate.

Technical difficulty: 2 on jeep trail; 3 on ATV-width singletrack.

Highlights: A very pleasant

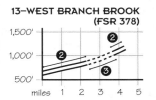

58

WEST BRANCH BROOK
Ride 13
PEAKED HILL POND TRAIL FROM WEST BRANCH BROOK
Ride 14

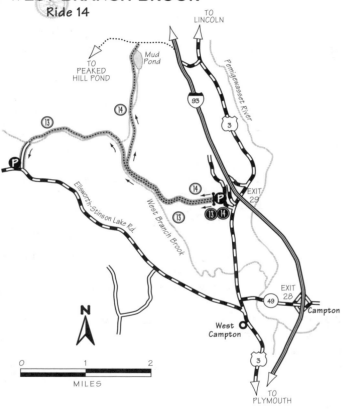

ride along the brook with beautiful waterfalls, swimming holes, and picnic spots. Look for moose in Ellsworth Bog.

Hazards: Some tricky stream crossings. Logging in this area over the next few years may change trail conditions.

Land status: White Mountain National Forest.

Maps: WMNF Mountain Bike Map; DeLorme New Hampshire Atlas and Gazetteer, 10th edition; AMC Map 4 Chocorua-Waterville Valley; USGS Plymouth and Woodstock quadrangles.

Access: From Interstate 93, exit 29, turn south on U.S. Highway 3. Go 0.3 mile, through the underpass, and turn right at the top of the hill onto Adams Farm Road. Go 0.4 mile to Forest Service Road 378, rising to the left just before Jason Farm Road forks off to the right. Park clear of traffic on Adams Farm Road. The ride begins as you climb from Adams Farm Road.

The ride

0.0   Climb Forest Service Road 378 into pine trees on jeep trail.

0.1   Go around the Forest Service gate and continue straight on the road.

0.3   Continue straight past a junction with a road to a log landing area, past a clearcut.

0.4   Continue straight, past an old logging road on the left.

0.5   Road reenters woods from clearcut.

0.7   Begin a moderate climb.

1.1   The climb eases.

1.3   West Branch Brook joins the left side of the road.

2.1   Cross a small wooden bridge.

2.2   Stay left with the brook at a Y intersection.

2.3   Ride around the earthen barrier to the right and continue on ATV-width singletrack trail.

2.4 The trail bends slightly to the right and climbs a short, moderate rise. Look for a good picnic spot to the left on a granite outcrop along the brook.

2.5 Stay left at the trail junction and climb the rise. This turn can be missed easily when screaming downhill on the return trip.

2.6 A really nice waterfall and swimming hole are on the left as you crest the rise.

2.7 The trail becomes more rocky. Watch out for the intermittent streambed. Level 3.

2.9 Cross a stream and pass a national forest boundary marker on the left.

3.1 Ride through a raspberry patch while watching out for bears in late July. Cross a stream to the right on O'Reagan Bridge (safer than it looks) and rejoin the trail.

3.3 Stream crossing.

3.4 The trail dips right and crosses a stream. The climb from the stream is slightly more technical. Use caution as the rocky outcrop on the far side can be slippery when wet.

3.5 Cross a slightly washed-out stream and climb through more technical terrain.

3.6 The trail levels out.

3.7 Stay left at an intersection.

3.8 Turn left as the trail joins a dirt road and riding becomes easier. Level 2.

4.0 The trail begins a slight descent by a camp driveway on the right.

4.1 Cross Ellsworth Bog Bridge over West Branch Brook, gaining fine views into Ellsworth Bog. Begin a moderate climb up and out of the bog.

4.2 Turn left onto Ellsworth Village Road (gravel) and begin a short grunt climb into Ellsworth Village.

4.4 The ride finishes at the Ellsworth Old Schoolhouse and Town Hall at the junction with Ellsworth–Stinson Lake Road.

Variation: You can make a loop out of this ride by returning on paved roads if you go left onto Ellsworth–Stinson Lake Road. Climb Ellsworth Hill (a 1.7-mile, grueling, why-the-heck-am-I-doing-this lung burner), which affords some of the nicest views in the area from its top. Pause to tune up your brakes and begin the 2.7-mile screaming descent. Turn left at the stop sign and left again at the bottom of the hill onto U.S. Highway 3 north. Go 1.3 miles and turn left onto Adams Farm Road, returning to the start. This ride can also be joined with the Ellsworth Pond ride (Ride 9).

Peaked Hill Pond from West Branch Brook

[See map page 59]

Location: 0.8 mile west of Interstate 93, exit 29, in the towns of Campton, Thornton, and Ellsworth.

Distance: 4.1-mile one way (5.7 miles all the way to the pond).

Time: 30 minutes to 1 hour.

Tread: 2.2 miles on dirt road; 0.5 mile on jeep trail; 1.4 miles on ATV-width doubletrack.

Aerobic level: Easy to moderate.

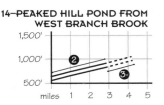

14–PEAKED HILL POND FROM WEST BRANCH BROOK

Technical difficulty: 2 on jeep trail; 3- on ATV-width doubletrack broken up by many sections of easier trail.

Highlights: A very nice ride on a good trail that has many smooth, nontechnical sections. The 3- technical rating is due to the rough sections caused by recent logging operations. This is a ride for beginners wishing to push into more technical terrain.

Hazards: Watch for logging traffic in the woods.

Land status: White Mountain National Forest.

Maps: USGS Woodstock and Plymouth quadrangles (trail not shown on map).

Access: From Interstate 93, exit 29, turn south on U.S. Highway 3. Go 0.3 mile, through the underpass, and turn right at the top of the hill onto Adams Farm Road. Go 0.4 mile to Forest Service Road 378, rising to the left just before Jason Farm Road forks off to the right. Park clear of traffic on Adams Farm Road. The ride begins as you climb from Adams Farm Road.

The ride

0.0   Climb Forest Service Road 378 into pine trees on jeep trail. Level 2.
0.1   Go around the Forest Service gate; continue straight on the road.
0.3   Continue straight past a junction with a road to a log landing area, past a clearcut.
0.4   Continue straight by an old logging road on the left.
0.5   Road reenters woods from clearcut.
0.7   Begin a moderate climb.
1.1   The climb eases.
1.3   West Branch Brook joins the left side of the road.
2.1   Cross a small wooden bridge.
2.2   Stay right at the Y intersection, following the main road

as it becomes narrower, grassy jeep trail. West Branch Brook (Ride 13) leaves to the left.

2.3 Stay right again on the main track and cross a concrete bridge.

2.7 Pass through a log landing and continue on the ATV-width doubletrack over several water bars. Recent logging has broken up the trail from here in many places. Level 3-.

3.0 Cross a stream on a dislodged bridge.

3.3 Traverse on the smooth old roadbed cut into the hillside.

3.5 Dip down to cross an intermittent stream over logs imbedded in the mud.

3.8 Pass an area that is often quite muddy before making a climb on loose rocks and dirt. Begin traversing the west side of Mud Pond below and to your right.

4.0 Begin a quick descent over bumpy trail.

4.1 Join Peaked Hill Pond Trail (Ride 14) at mile 0.6. To continue to the pond, see variation below.

Variation: Join this ride with Peaked Hill Pond Trail (Ride 24) to continue to the pond. Turn left and follow the description from mile 0.6.

Chandler Hill Road

Location: 2.4 miles west of Interstate 93, exit 28, in Campton.

Distance: 10.2-mile loop.

Time: 1.5 to 2 hours.

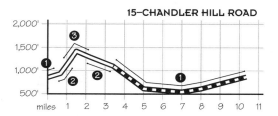

15–CHANDLER HILL ROAD

Tread: 1.8 miles on jeep trail; 1.4 miles on dirt road; 7.0 miles on paved road.

Aerobic level: Moderate because of a steep climb at the beginning of Chandler Hill Road. The downhill on the other side easily makes it worthwhile if you aren't partial to hill climbing.

Technical difficulty: 1 on paved roads; 2 on dirt roads; 2 and 3 on jeep trail.

Highlights: A good climb past scenic farm fields on Chandler Hill Road. A great descent from Chandler Hill with two options (see mile 2.3 and the Variation below).

Hazards: Watch for traffic on U.S. Highway 3.

Land status: Town roads.

Maps: DeLorme New Hampshire Atlas and Gazetteer, 10th edition; USGS Plymouth Quadrangle.

Access: From Interstate 93, exit 28, go west onto Bog Road. Go 4.2 miles and turn left onto Beech Hill Road. Park near Rowbartwood Pond. Do not block the red fire hydrant pipe at the far side of the dam. The ride begins from the intersection of Beech Hill Road and Bog Road.

The ride

0.0   From the intersection of Bog Road and Beech Hill Road, ride northwest (left) on Bog Road.

CHANDLER HILL ROAD
Ride 15
CHANDLER HILL POWER RUN
Ride 16

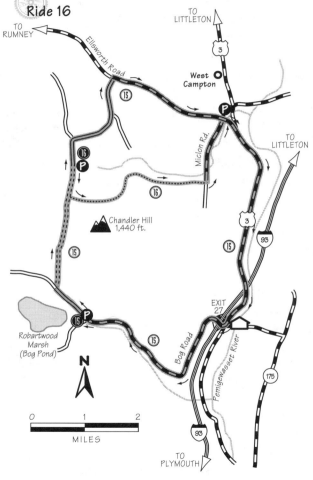

TO LITTLETON

3

West Campton

TO RUMNEY

Ellsworth Road

15

P

16

P

16

Miclon Rd.

TO LITTLETON

Chandler Hill
1,440 ft.

3

93

15

15

EXIT 27

15

P

15

Robartwood Marsh
(Bog Pond)

Bog Road

Pemigewasset River

175

N

0   1   2
MILES

93

TO PLYMOUTH

0.2 The road turns to dirt.

0.5 Just past a sugar shack on the right, turn right onto Chandler Hill Road, marked with a "Road Closed" sign. Climb steeply up the sand and gravel jeep trail with a grassy center. Level 2.

1.0 The climb relents as you continue past fields onto more overgrown and rutted track. Level 3.

1.2 Pass a snowmobile trail on the left.

1.3 Cross an intermittent stream and begin a moderate climb.

1.6 Continue through a trail junction marked with several snowmobile signs and a trail map on the left. The trail to the right is the Chandler Hill Power Run (Ride 16; see Variation below).

1.9 Descend past a logging road that is gated with a cable on the left.

2.1 Pass a pullout on the right and begin climbing past several driveways on improved road. Level 2.

2.3 At the end of Chandler Hill Road, turn right onto Mason Road (not marked) and begin a long descent to West Campton. If you wish to cut the ride short, making an out-and-back ride, this is the best place to turn around.

2.5 Mason Road becomes paved for a short distance.

2.8 Pass Quimby Road on the right as the road bends left and returns to dirt.

3.4 At the stop sign, turn right onto Ellsworth Road (paved) and admire the view to the left as you coast past the Armont Inn. Level 1.

4.9 Stop at the stop sign to cool your brakes before turning right onto Dan Web Road, past Avery's General Store.

5.1 Stay right at the stop sign onto U.S. Highway 3 south. Watch out for fast-moving traffic!

7.1 Pass under Interstate 93.

7.7 At the blinking light, turn right onto Bog Road and pass under Interstate 93 again.

10.2 You're at Beech Hill Road again.

Variation: You can turn onto Chandler Hill Power Run (Ride 16) at mile 1.6 and have an off-road descent of Chandler Hill, rejoining the ride at mile 4.9.

Chandler Hill Power Run

[See map page 66]

Location: 4.2 miles west of Interstate 93, exit 28, in Campton.

Distance: 3.3-mile one way.

Time: 30 minutes to 1 hour.

Tread: 0.6 mile on jeep trail; 2.2 miles on ATV-width single track; 0.1 mile on dirt road; 0.4 mile on paved road.

16–CHANDLER HILL POWER RUN

Aerobic level: Easy to moderate, mostly downhill.

Technical difficulty: 1 on dirt road and paved road; 2 on jeep trail; 3 and 3+ on ATV-width singletrack.

Highlights: A fast, downhill run with technical challenge.

Hazards: Watch for heavy traffic on U.S. Highway 3. Also try to avoid clamper cramps from excessive braking.

Land status: Private lands and town roads.

Maps: USGS Plymouth Quadrangle (trail not shown on map).

Access: From Interstate 93, take exit 28. Go west at the bottom of the ramp on New Hampshire 49 and go 1.1 miles, passing under the overpass. To leave a shuttle car, turn right (north) on U.S. Highway 3 and park immediately on the left in a dirt pull-out across from the Sunset Grill. Take your bikes on the second car on U.S. Highway 3 south (less than a tenth of a mile) and turn right on Dan Web Road just past the intersection with New Hampshire 49. At the top of the rise, turn right again onto Ellsworth Hill Road. Go 1.4 miles and turn left after the Armont Inn onto Mason Road (dirt). Go 1.1 miles and turn left onto Chandler Hill Road. (Stay to the right at 0.6 mile, following Mason Road as it becomes paved.) Go 0.2 mile and park in a pullout on the left. There is room for two cars. The ride begins as you continue down Chandler Hill Road past an old, rusty, red fire truck.

The ride

0.0   Continue south on Chandler Hill Road, past the more-rust-than-red fire truck. The road becomes jeep trail with a grassy center as you soon begin an easy-to-moderate climb into the woods. Level 2.

0.3   Pass a cutoff on the right blocked by a cable as the trail levels off.

0.6   Turn left at the junction marked by several snowmobile trail signs on the right, including a red stop sign and trail map. Turn left on new trail called "Power Run." The trail becomes ATV width and is washed out as you make a short descent followed by a gradual climb. Level 3.

0.8   The trail levels off for a while as you begin to navigate a series of soft, muddy holes.

1.0 Fasten your safety belts: It's all downhill from here! Don't get too out of control as there are obstacles in the trail. Level 3+.

1.5 Stay left following the arrow at the trail junction as the woods open a little and you ride through grass and ferns.

1.8 Pay heed to the "Caution" sign as you drop into a washed-out section of trail. Turn right at the junction marked by arrows and continue the descent.

2.0 Watch out for the gully before crossing a bridge and riding into a smooth section of trail through a hemlock grove.

2.3 Enter a small clearing in a marshy area before making a stream crossing that is fairly deep and often has pallets bridging it.

2.8 Emerge onto Miclon Road (dirt). Turn left and continue descending. Level 1.

2.9 Follow Miclon Road across a bridge and past a house on the left (the dog is usually on a rope!). The road soon becomes paved as you pass White House Circle to the right.

3.2 Turn left onto Dan Web Road and descend to U.S. Highway 3.

3.3 Watch for traffic as you turn left, going north on U.S. Highway 3, and return to your shuttle vehicle on the left across from the Sunset Grill.

Variations: If you only have one vehicle you can ride the whole trip as a loop and really earn the fun of the descent. Also, this ride can be combined with the Chandler Hill Road ride (Ride 15).

Sandwich Notch Road

Location: 5.5 miles east of Interstate 93, exit 28, on New Hampshire 49 in Campton.

Distance: 8.8-mile one way.

Time: 1 to 2 hours.

Tread: 1.1 miles on paved road; 7.7 miles on dirt road.

Aerobic level: Moderate to strenuous.

Technical difficulty: 1 on paved road; 2 on dirt road.

Highlights: This is a very scenic ride on a seasonal road with a rich history. An early trade route that once connected the seacoast to the north country, Sandwich Notch Road has remained essentially unchanged in location and character since the eighteenth century. There are climbs and descents with many ride options (see Variations below). Keep an eye out for wildlife.

Hazards: Conditions change from year to year.

Land status: White Mountain National Forest.

Maps: WMNF Mountain Bike Map; DeLorme New Hampshire Atlas and Gazetteer, 10th edition; USGS Waterville Valley,

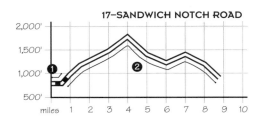

17–SANDWICH NOTCH ROAD

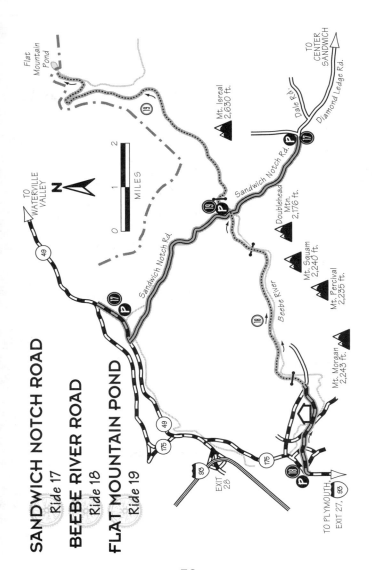

SANDWICH NOTCH ROAD
Ride 17

BEEBE RIVER ROAD
Ride 18

FLAT MOUNTAIN POND
Ride 19

72

Squam Mountains, and Mount Chocorua quadrangles.

Access: This ride can be done in either direction but is described from Campton to Sandwich. If you wish to ride it only one way, you need to leave a car at the other end. To get to the Campton end from Interstate 93 north, exit 28, go east (right) on New Hampshire 49 for 5.2 miles to the Smarts Brook parking area on the right, where there is parking for about 15 cars. The ride begins by leaving the parking area and heading west on New Hampshire 49.

To get to the Sandwich end, drive across Sandwich Notch Road, the same route the ride follows if your vehicle has good clearance, or from Interstate 93, exit 24, go 4.5 miles on U.S. Highway 3 south/New Hampshire 25 east, through Ashland (bear left at 0.7 mile). Turn east (left) onto New Hampshire 113 in Holderness and go 11.6 miles to Center Sandwich. Turn sharply left at the first road opposite the AG Burrows General Store onto Grove Street (Diamond Ledge Road). Go 2.4 miles (stay left past Mount Isreal Road, 0.4 mile), to a Y. Sandwich Notch Road goes left, and you can park at a pullout on the left just past the Y intersection.

The ride

0.0 Ride west on New Hampshire 49 from the west exit of the Smarts Brook parking area.

0.8 Turn left onto Sandwich Notch Road and begin a long, strenuous climb. Level 2.

1.1 The road surface changes to dirt as the climb briefly relents. This might be a good place to pause and put your lungs back in your chest before continuing the climb.

1.5 Pass the trailhead for Chickenboro Brook (Ride 20).

1.6 Pass West Meadow Road on the left as you ride into a meadow with excellent views to the northeast. Good job on the climb!

1.8	Just past an old barn, drop down into the woods and begin climbing again.
2.1	Pass the Atwood Trail (Ride 22) parking area and go by the "Historic Sandwich Notch Road Established 1801, Entering White Mountain National Forest" sign.
2.4	Pass the Atwood Pond (Ride 23) cutoff on your left.
2.5	The climbing levels off.
2.8	Climb on a short paved stretch of road.
3.0	Make your way up a short steep pitch.
3.2	A road descends right to Hall Pond (0.3 mile).
3.6	A descent(!), paved partway.
4.2	As the road levels, pass a house on the right.
4.3	Cross a bridge.
4.4	Pass the Algonquin Trailhead.
4.5	Climb sharply at first, then easing.
5.6	Begin another descent.
5.8	Pass under powerlines and cross an intersection. Beebe River Road (Ride 18) ends on the right, and Kiah Pond, a nice side trip, is 0.8 mile to the left. Continue over the one-lane bridge.
5.9	Climb past the Guinea Pond Trailhead, start of the Flat Mountain Pond ride (Ride 19).
6.1	A brief pause in the climb. Are your legs burning yet?
6.4	The climb eases.
6.6	Descend sharply over a short paved section.
7.2	Cross a bridge at the bottom of the steep descent.
7.4	Cross two consecutive bridges with large boulders to the left.
7.6	Pass the Crawford Ridgepole Trail on the right.
7.8	Leave White Mountain National Forest and continue descending.
8.0	Descend steeply on a section of paved road.
8.1	Pass the parking area for Sandwich Notch Park on the left; there is a nice cascade here.
8.3	Follow the road as it bends sharply left.

8.8   Reach the intersection with Diamond Ledge Road, the end of Sandwich Notch Road and the ride.

Variations: Incorporate this ride with Beebe River Road (Ride 18), Flat Mountain Pond (Ride 19), Chickenboro Brook (Ride 20), Atwood Trail (Ride 22), or Atwood Pond (Ride 23).

Beebe River Road

[See map page 72]

Location: 1.4 miles east of Interstate 93, exit 27, in Campton.

Distance: 8.7-mile one way.

Time: 2 to 3 hours.

Tread: 2.3 miles on paved road; 7.3 miles on dirt road.

Aerobic level: Moderate with some steep climbing at the beginning.

Technical difficulty: 1 on paved roads; 2 to 3 on dirt roads.

Highlights: A fairly easy ride on old road along the Beebe River. You get to cross a covered bridge.

Land status: Private land; White Mountain National Forest.

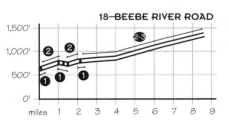

Maps: WMNF Mountain Bike Map; DeLorme New Hampshire Atlas and Gazetteer, 10th edition; USGS Plymouth and Squam Mountains quadrangles.

Access: From Interstate 93, exit 27, go east, 0.8 mile, through the blinking light at U.S. Highway 3 onto Blair Road and across Blair Covered Bridge to New Hampshire 175. Go north (left) 0.6 mile to the old Campton Town Hall and Library, on the left, and park in the lot. The ride begins as you pedal north on New Hampshire 175.

The ride

0.0   Go north on New Hampshire 175.
0.1   Turn at the second right, ascending steeply on Hog Back Road (dirt).
1.0   At the stop sign, turn right onto Perch Pond Road (paved).
1.5   Cross the covered bridge to the left on Bump's Intervale Road (dirt).
2.0   The road becomes paved as you begin a long climb.
2.2   Bear right at the fork.
2.3   Road becomes dirt.
2.4   Stay straight, cresting the hill past Avery Road and then descending.
2.6   Pass a small graveyard on the left.
2.7   Turn left onto Beebe River Road (unmarked).
2.9   Pass a steel gate and continue on Beebe River Road. Do not diverge from this road for the rest of the ride.
3.0   Join the Beebe River on the right.
5.0   Pass an old building foundation on the left.
6.0   Cross a bridge.
6.2   Ride through loose rocks and gravel.
6.4   Stay on the rocky road past a road to the left.

6.9 Stay left past a road branching to the right across a bridge.

7.6 Pass around the Forest Service gate and stay right at the fork in the road.

7.7 Pass the national forest boundary marker on the left.

8.1 Stay right past a road on the left, gated at the far side of the powerlines.

8.2 Cross a wooden bridge.

8.7 Meet Sandwich Notch Road at a four-way intersection. This is the end of the ride. Return the way you came or see Variations below.

Variations: Connect this ride to Flat Mountain Pond (Ride 19) by turning right; the trailhead is over the bridge on the left. You can also ride on Sandwich Notch Road (Ride 17).

Flat Mountain Pond

[See map page 72]

Location: 9.3 miles east of Interstate 93, exit 28, in Sandwich.

Distance: 8.2-mile one way.

Time: 2 to 3 hours one way.

Tread: 7.7 miles on ATV-width doubletrack (old railroad bed); 0.5 mile on singletrack.

Aerobic level: Moderate as you climb an old railroad bed.

Technical difficulty: 2 to 3, 3 to 4, and 5 on ATV-width doubletrack; 3+ and 4 on singletrack.

Highlights: One of the more scenic rides with excellent wildlife viewing, cascading waterfalls, an excellent pond view, and great swimming. The trail follows the upper portion of the Old Beebe River Railroad Bed; the lower portion of the old railroad bed follows what is now Beebe River Road (Ride 18). The "Great Horseshoe" curve at mile 5.7 was about the sharpest switchback ever constructed on a White Mountains logging railroad. As you ride this trail, imagine the life of loggers as they pushed their way into this wilderness 70 or 80 years ago.

Hazards: Sandwich Notch Road is not maintained for winter travel and should only be driven with vehicles having good clearance. See Variations below for other routes giving access to this one.

Land status: White Mountain National Forest.

Maps: WMNF Mountain Bike Map; DeLorme New Hampshire Atlas and Gazetteer, 10th edition; USGS Squam Mountains and Mount Chocorua quadrangles.

Access: From Interstate 93, take exit 28. Go east at the bottom of the ramp on New Hampshire 49 toward Waterville Valley for 4.2 miles. Turn right onto Sandwich Notch Road, ascending past the "Be Careful with Fire" sign. Follow this road 5.1 miles to the Guinea Pond Trailhead, on the left just under the powerlines, and over the bridge crossing the Beebe River. Park

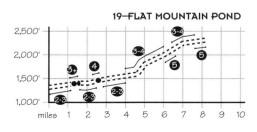

78

along the trailhead off Sandwich Notch Road, being careful not to block access to the gate. The ride begins as you pass the Forest Service gate at the end of the trailhead.

The ride

0.0 Pass around the Forest Service gate and ride under the powerlines, following the Guinea Pond Trail on ATV-width doubletrack trail. Level 2 to 3 with a challenging Level 4 ride into the woods over loose grapefruit-sized rocks.

0.2 Ascend through a severe washout; watch this one on your way out! The trail is more recognizable now as an old railbed with sand and gravel.

0.9 Pass a small boggy clearing as the trail becomes more grassy.

1.1 Pass a steel Forest Service gate.

1.2 Stay right at the Y intersection (unless you brought your water wings). The trail climbs on singletrack to the right from the railbed around a beaver pond.

1.3 Cross an intermittent stream just before riding a ledgy outcrop.

1.4 At the end of the beaver pond the trail turns right, away from the water. Cross three narrow wooden bridges. Level 3+.

1.5 Stay right on ATV-width doubletrack trail, following a sign for the Guinea Pond Trail. In 40 yards, pass through the intersection of the Mead Trail on the right and the Black Mountain Pond Trail on the left. Cross an intermittent stream. Level 2 to 3.

1.6 Cross a stream that could be troublesome in high water (alternately, look for a narrow singletrack to the right, avoiding this and the next crossing). In a short distance, ride over a small ledge outcrop and cross the stream again on gravel.

1.7 Cross the stream again over rocks. In 50 yards, continue past a singletrack splitting off to the left.

2.3 Drop down into a washed-out, sloppy, muddy hollow. Level 4.

2.4 As you climb from the hollow, don't follow the obvious path. Go left following the yellow arrow onto a new singletrack trail skirting the left edge of a bog.

2.6 Cross a split-log bridge and regain the ATV-width doubletrack railbed to the left. Level 2 to 3.

2.8 Cross the stream on large boulders.

3.2 Use caution as you dip down, crossing a small stream on a wooden bridge washed out at both ends.

3.3 Cross an intermittent stream on large rocks.

3.5 Traverse a section of trail broken by roots and logs imbedded in mud.

3.8 Cross a wooden bridge.

4.0 Pass the Jose's Bridge and Bennett Street trails descending to the right. A variation for the return (see Variations below) rejoins the trail here. The trail becomes steeper and more rocky. Level 3 to 4.

4.7 Cross an intermittent stream.

5.0 Have your granny gears ready for the steep climb on the opposite side as you descend into a steep ravine with a rocky stream crossing at the bottom. A round of drinks to the person who makes it up the other side.

5.1 Pass the Gleason Trail (marked by a white sign on a birch tree), that climbs to Mount Sandwich on the left, and descend to Jose's Bridge to the right, where the variation for the return leaves down the hill (see Variations below). Note that the Sandwich Range Wilderness Area boundary is to the left up the hill; mountain biking is not allowed in wilderness areas.

5.4 Ride on washed-out trail.

5.6 Crest a rise on irritating remnant railroad ties imbedded in the mud. Pass the Bennett Street Trail.

5.7 Cross the cascading stream on large boulders. This is the "Great Horseshoe" curve in the old railroad line.

6.1 Climb over washed-out trail with many large, loose rocks. Level 5.

6.2 The trail improves. Level 3 to 4.

6.4 Dip down to a challenging stream crossing on large, loose rock.

6.6 Try your skill on this boulder-infested section of trail. Level 5.

6.7 Carry across a stream on boulders to the left, or challenge the water. In 50 yards, recross the stream. Level 3 to 4.

6.9 Cross the stream.

7.0 Pass through a beaver bog, climbing the far side on washed-out, rocky trail. Level 5.

7.2 The trail improves. Level 3 to 4.

7.5 As you climb through young hemlock trees, look for sections of old steel rail, which are remnants of the Beebe River Railroad. Most of the rails were removed in 1942 to support the war effort.

7.9 Climb over loose rock of varying size and steepness. Level 5.

8.0 Stay to the left at this rocky, marshy stream crossing.

8.1 Turn right at a trail junction, following the sign to the shelter.

8.2 Arrive at the shelter with a beautiful view of Flat Mountain Pond.

Variation 1: Continue east around the pond on Flat Mountain Pond Trail by turning left at mile 8.1. The railroad bed ends and the trail becomes considerably more difficult, but improves again as you near Whiteface Intervale.

Variation 2: Returning from the shelter, drop down on the Gleason Trail toward Jose's Bridge at mile 5.1. Stay right until you come to an old logging road that climbs back to the Flat Mountain Pond Trail, regaining it at mile 4.0.

Variation 3: Join this ride with Beebe River Road (Ride 18) for a full-day ride or with the Sandwich Notch Road ride (Ride 17).

Chickenboro Brook

Location: 4.9 miles from Interstate 93, exit 28, off Sandwich Notch Road in Campton.

Distance: 4.2-mile loop.

Time: 45 minutes to 1.25 hours.

Tread: 1.5 miles of smooth, grassy jeep trail; 1.1 miles of ATV-width singletrack; 0.8 mile on dirt road; 0.8 mile on paved roads.

Aerobic level: Moderate with one strenuous climb at the end.

Technical difficulty: 1 on jeep trail, dirt and paved roads; 3 on ATV-width singletrack with one section (0.1 mile) of 4.

Highlights: A great gliding ride on a grassy Forest Service road lined with ferns and wildflowers. The ride along Chickenboro Brook takes you through some classic New Hampshire mossy forest.

Hazards: The route finding is a bit tricky and requires a short bushwhack at Chickenboro Brook. Also be aware of fast-moving traffic on New Hampshire 49.

20–CHICKENBORO BROOK

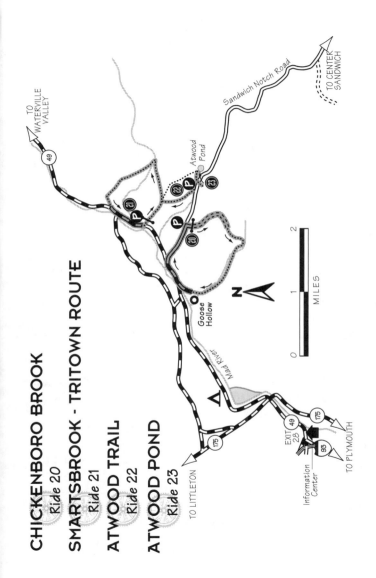

CHICKENBORO BROOK
Ride 20

SMARTSBROOK - TRITOWN ROUTE
Ride 21

ATWOOD TRAIL
Ride 22

ATWOOD POND
Ride 23

83

Land status: White Mountain National Forest and town roads.

Maps: WMNF Mountain Bike Map; USGS Squam Mountains and Waterville Valley quadrangles.

Access: From Interstate 93, exit 28, go east at the bottom of the ramp on New Hampshire 49 toward Waterville Valley for 4.2 miles. Turn right onto Sandwich Notch Road, ascending past the "Be Careful with Fire" sign. Follow this road 0.7 mile to the trailhead at gated Forest Service Road 206 on the right. Park at the trailhead, being careful not to block the gate. The ride begins as you pass around the gate on Forest Service Road 206.

The ride

0.0   Pass around the green Forest Service gate and begin a steady, gradual climb on the grassy, open road lined with ferns and wildflowers. This is actually the upper part of Chickenboro Road, now known as Forest Service Road 206. Level 1.

0.8   Continue as you reach the top of the rise and descend to a large open field.

1.4   Follow the trail as it swings right into and across the large, grassy, open field. Exit the field on the far side by crossing an earthen mound and descend to Chickenboro Brook.

1.5   The road dead ends at Chickenboro Brook where the trail has been washed out. Do not cross the brook. Look for an overgrown, difficult-to-find, and narrow trail opening to the right. It's a bit of a bushwhack for about 25 yards down the brook's near bank until you come to the trail again. From here, the trail is a beautiful, dark, and mossy ATV-width singletrack that follows the brook's right shoulder.

1.7   Ford Chickenboro Brook. It may be hard to keep your

feet dry in high water. Continue on the far side down the brook, traversing large rocks and logs, through a section of trail that has been badly washed out, for about 50 yards. All but expert riders will probably have to carry this section. The trail again becomes rideable. Level 3.

1.9 More difficult washed-out trail. Carry or try your luck on these rocks and roots.

2.3 Note the cairn of red stones on the right that marks a land survey monument.

2.5 Descend the trail, which looks more like a streambed at this point. It is often wet with loose, grapefruit-sized rocks. Go past a shack set back on the left; this is the only section of Level 4.

2.6 Pass a camp on the left as the trail improves and re-crosses Chickenboro Brook on a snowmobile bridge. Follow the dirt road after the bridge. Level 1.

2.7 The road improves with a gravel surface as you pass some houses on the right. This is the top of Chickenboro Road; follow it down to Goose Hollow.

2.8 Stay right as you pass the entrance to Waterville Estates (paved) on the left.

3.0 Bear right onto the paved surface.

3.1 Turn right at the stop sign onto New Hampshire 49. Be cautious of fast-moving traffic.

3.5 Follow Sandwich Notch Road to the right and begin a long, strenuous climb back to the trailhead.

3.8 The road surface changes to dirt as the climb briefly relents. This might be a good place to pause and put your lungs back in your chest before continuing the climb.

4.2 Arrive at the trailhead. Good job on the climb!

Smarts Brook– Tritown Route

[See map page 83]

Location: 5.5 miles east of Interstate 93, exit 28, on New Hampshire 49, beginning in Campton.

Distance: 3.5-mile loop.

Time: 30 minutes to 1 hour.

Tread: 0.6 mile on paved road; 0.6 mile on jeep trail; 0.7 mile on ATV-width singletrack; 1.6 miles on singletrack.

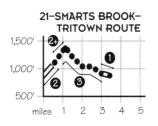

21–SMARTS BROOK– TRITOWN ROUTE

Aerobic level: A moderate climb for 1.2 miles, followed by downhill runs.

Technical difficulty: 1 on paved road; 2 on jeep trail; 2+ and 3 on singletrack.

Highlights: The area trails are in the Smarts Brook Ski Area and consist of five scenic trails of varying difficulty. The easy access to this short ride makes it ideal for those who want a quick ride when schedules are tight. The loop described covers three of the trails.

Hazards: Watch out for fast-moving traffic on New Hampshire 49.

Land status: White Mountain National Forest.

Maps: WMNF Mountain Bike Map; WMNF "Cross Country Skiing Smarts/Brook Ski Trails" handout (available at the information center, Interstate 93, at exit 28); USGS Waterville Valley Quadrangle (not all trails shown).

Access: From Interstate 93, exit 28, go east on New Hampshire 49 for 5.2 miles to the Smarts Brook parking area on the right, where there is parking for about 15 cars. The ride begins by leaving the parking area on New Hampshire 49 west.

The ride

0.0 Leave the parking area and go west (left) on New Hampshire 49, crossing over Smarts Brook.

0.1 Take the first left and climb onto a Forest Service road that is paved for the first few hundred feet. Go around the Forest Service gate and continue a gradual climb into the woods; this is the Smarts Brook Trail.

0.3 Turn right onto the Tritown Trail (named because it traverses portions of the towns of Sandwich, Thornton, and Waterville Valley) and continue the gradual climb on the old roadbed.

0.4 Continue past a clearing on the right as the trail narrows to ATV-width singletrack.

0.5 The trail bends to the left and descends slightly.

0.6 Begin a gradual climb with a slight increase in trail difficulty. Level 2+.

0.8 Pass through a small clearing.

1.0 Trail becomes singletrack and increases in technical difficulty with rocks, roots, and ruts. Level 3.

1.2 Begin a descent.

1.4 Cross a wooden bridge at the bottom of the hill and rejoin the Smarts Brook Trail (doubletrack jeep trail). Turn right and ride on.

1.5	Turn left, cross Smarts Brook on a large wooden bridge, and immediately turn left at the Y intersection onto the mostly descending, singletrack Yellow Jacket Trail. Level 3.
1.6	Cross a plastic culvert pipe and ride up a short hill.
1.7	Begin descending again.
2.1	Challenge the mud in a boggy area or avoid it by a spur trail to the right.
2.2	Cross a small wooden bridge and climb as the trail difficulty eases.
2.4	Begin descending again.
2.5	Cross a wooden bridge.
2.7	Stay right as the Pine Flat Trail (one way) enters from the left. Turn left in a short distance at the intersection with the Old Waterville Road (signposted).
2.8	Turn sharply left and use caution as you cross a wooden bridge that can be mossy and slippery. Ascend on the right-sloping trail after the bridge.
2.9	Begin a quick descent to New Hampshire 49.
3.0	Turn left and ride on New Hampshire 49 (paved) back to the parking area.
3.5	Back at Smarts Brook parking area.

Variation: Extend the loop by turning right at the junction with the Old Waterville Road. At the High Brook Picnic Area, turn left and return to the parking area on paved New Hampshire 49. You can also access this trail from the Atwood Trail (Ride 22).

Atwood Trail

[See map page 83]

Location: 5.4 miles east of Interstate 93, exit 28, off Sandwich Notch Road in Campton.

Distance: 0.7-mile one way.

Time: 10 to 30 minutes.

Tread: 0.7 mile on singletrack.

Aerobic level: Easy; it's all downhill; strenuous if you have to climb back up.

22–ATWOOD TRAIL

Technical difficulty: 3 and 5- on singletrack.

Highlights: An excellent, technical downhill ride that accesses the Smarts Brook area.

Land status: White Mountain National Forest.

Maps: USGS Waterville Valley Quadrangle (trail not shown).

Access: From Interstate 93, take exit 28. Go east at the bottom of the ramp, on New Hampshire 49, toward Waterville Valley for 4.2 miles. Turn right onto Sandwich Notch Road, ascending past the "Be Careful with Fire" sign. Follow this road 1.2 miles to the trailhead, a small pullout on the left within sight of a sign that reads, "Historic Sandwich Notch Road Established 1801, Entering White Mountain National Forest." The ride begins from the back of the pullout, to the left of a trail map posted on a tree.

The ride

0.0   Begin descending singletrack from the back of the pull-out, to the left of a trail map posted on a tree. Level 5-.

0.1   A short distance after the brook joins the right side of the trail, cross to the other side. Look for the blue-diamond ski-trail marker.

0.4   After a particularly difficult section, the trail opens a bit to a wide, grassy corridor. Level 3.

0.6   Cross several water bars and an intermittent stream.

0.7   Emerge into a clearing as you join the Tritown Trail on the Smarts Brook–Tritown Route (Ride 21).

Variation: To make a great loop out of this ride, turn right, following the Tritown Trail (Ride 21, Smarts Brook–Tritown Route) from mile 0.8. When you get to the Smarts Brook Trail parking area, continue west on New Hampshire 49 for 0.9 mile and turn left onto Sandwich Notch Road. Ascend past the "Be Careful with Fire" sign and climb the lung-bustin' hill 1.2 miles to the trailhead. You can also start by parking at the Smarts Brook Trailhead and climbing Sandwich Notch Road first, finishing at your car with a downhill.

Atwood Pond

[See map page 83]

Location: 5.4 miles east of Interstate 93, exit 28, off Sandwich Notch Road in Campton.

Distance: 0.7-mile one way.

Time: 15 to 45 minutes.

Tread: 0.3 mile on dirt road; 0.4 mile on singletrack.

23–ATWOOD POND

Aerobic level: Easy, after the moderate 0.3-mile climb up Sandwich Notch Road.

Technical difficulty: 1 on dirt road; 3 on singletrack.

Highlights: A short ride to a pretty pond with potential for wildlife viewing and swimming.

Land status: White Mountain National Forest.

Maps: USGS Waterville Valley Quadrangle (trail not shown).

Access: From Interstate 93, take exit 28. Go east at the bottom of the ramp on New Hampshire 49, toward Waterville Valley, for 4.2 miles. Turn right onto Sandwich Notch Road, ascending past the "Be Careful with Fire" sign. Follow this road 1.2 miles to the trailhead, a small pullout on the left within sight of a sign that reads, "Historic Sandwich Notch Road, Established 1801, Entering White Mountain National Forest." The ride begins by turning left, back onto Sandwich Notch Road, and continuing to climb from the parking pullout.

The ride

0.0   From the parking pullout, go back onto Sandwich Notch Road, turn left, and begin a steady climb on the dirt road. Level 1.

0.2   Pass a small pullout on the left.

0.3   Turn left into a pullout and ride out the back on singletrack, through a large log that has been cut in half. Level 3.

0.4   Climb the left side of the trail past a washout. Turn left at an overgrown clearing and descend between two close birch trees to a stream crossing at the base of a beaver dam. Look for a blue ski-trail diamond on the right-hand tree. As you cross the stream, look up to the dam and check out the huge, mossy log on the right, a relic from the past.

0.6   Stay right past a trail cutting back to the left, continuing past the "Atwood Pond" sign.

0.7   Arrive at the backwaters of Atwood Pond. A small foot trail goes left to better views of the pond.

Variations: At mile 0.6, the trail cutting back to the left is very overgrown and difficult to follow, but it connects to the junctions of the Smarts Brook–Tritown Route (Ride 21) at mile 0.8 and the end of the Atwood Trail (Ride 22). If you choose to put on your Lewis and Clark hats and push through, you can loop back to the start by climbing up the Atwood Trail in reverse.

Peaked Hill Pond Trail

Location: 2.8 miles west of Interstate 93, exit 29, in Thornton.

Distance: 1.7-mile one way.

Time: 30 minutes to 1 hour.

Tread: 1.6 miles on jeep trail; 0.1 mile on ATV-width singletrack.

Aerobic level: Easy to moderate.

Technical difficulty: 2 on jeep trail and ATV-width singletrack.

Highlights: This is a very pleasant ride through the woods on good trail. Peaked Hill Pond is a beautiful body of clear water nestled into the hills, edged by waterlilies, and teeming with dragonflies.

Land status: White Mountain National Forest at start of ride and private land at end.

Maps: WMNF Mountain Bike Map; DeLorme New Hampshire Atlas and Gazetteer, 10th edition; AMC Map 4 Chocorua-Waterville Valley; USGS Woodstock Quadrangle.

Access: From Interstate 93, exit 29, turn north onto U.S. Highway 3 and go 2.2 miles. Turn left onto Peaked Hill Pond Road just before the 93 Motel; note the Forest Service sign for the Peaked Hill Pond Trail. Follow the road 0.7 mile, passing

PEAKED HILL POND TRAIL
Ride 24
BAGLEY BROOK
Ride 25

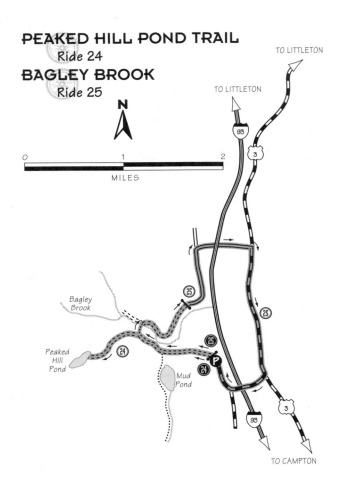

TO LITTLETON

TO LITTLETON

N

0   1   2

MILES

93

3

Bagley
Brook

25

25

Peaked
Hill
Pond

24

25

P

24

Mud
Pond

93

3

TO CAMPTON

under Interstate 93 (0.3 mile) and bearing right past Lumber Drive (0.4 mile) to the green Forest Service gate. Park along the road near the gate, being careful not to block the gate. Parking is limited here. Please do not block access to or park in the 93 Motel lot. The ride begins as you pass the Forest Service gate.

The ride

0.0 Pass around the Forest Service gate, and climb up and to the left on the Forest Service road's sandy surface, climbing through an old sugar orchard.

0.3 Cross the boundary into White Mountain National Forest.

0.5 At a junction, follow the older trail through a hemlock grove alongside the steep hill, or follow the more used road by staying to the left through a large, grassy field.

0.6 The trails rejoin and continue on a grassy jeep trail. If you follow the left option through the field, you will see a trail entering from the left just as the trails rejoin. This is where the Peaked Hill Pond Trail from West Branch Brook (Ride 14) ends.

0.9 Climb the grassy trail past a sharp left turn. This is where the Bagley Brook ride (Ride 25) diverges to the right. Continue over several water bars as the climb steepens.

1.5 The trail again separates. The left branch is very overgrown and the right one stays grassy and passes through a clearing. Either will do as they come together again on the far side of the clearing.

1.6 Stay right, leaving the jeep trail for the more narrow, overgrown trail as it rapidly descends to the pond's edge.

1.7 Arrive at the edge of Peaked Hill Pond in a pine tree-shaded campsite. Note that Peaked Hill Pond is privately owned. Please respect the rights of the landowner. Return on the same trail.

Variations: You can extend this ride by beginning on the Peaked Hill Pond Trail from West Branch Brook (Ride 14), then follow this description from mile 0.6. A return loop can be made by following Bagley Brook (Ride 25) from mile 0.9 of this description.

Bagley Brook

[See map page 94]

Location: 2.8 miles west of Interstate 93, exit 29, in Thornton.

Distance: 5.6-mile loop.

Time: 30 minutes to 1 hour.

Tread: 0.2 mile on ATV-width singletrack; 2.1 miles on jeep trail; 1.2 miles on dirt road; 2.1 miles on paved road.

Aerobic level: Easy to moderate.

Technical difficulty: 3 on ATV-width singletrack; 2 on jeep trail and dirt road; 1 on paved road.

Highlights: A nice downhill run on easy terrain and a great way to extend the Peaked Hill Pond Trail ride (Ride 24).

Hazards: Watch for traffic on U.S. Highway 3.

Land status: White Mountain National Forest, private and town roads.

Maps: WMNF Mountain Bike Map; DeLorme New Hampshire Atlas and Gazetteer, 10th edition; USGS Woodstock Quadrangle.

Access: From Interstate 93, exit 29, turn north onto U.S. Highway 3 and go 2.2 miles. Turn left onto Peaked Hill Pond Road just before the 93 Motel; note the Forest Service sign for the Peaked Hill Pond Trail. Follow the road 0.6 mile, passing under Interstate 93 in 0.3 mile and bearing right past Lumber Drive in 0.4 mile, to the green Forest Service gate. Park along the road near the gate, being careful not to block it. Parking is limited here. Please do not block access to or park in the 93 Motel lot. The ride begins as you pass the Forest Service gate.

The ride

0.0   Pass around the Forest Service gate and climb up and to the left on the Forest Service road's sandy surface, climbing through an old sugar orchard.

0.3   Cross the boundary into White Mountain National Forest.

0.5   At a junction, follow the older trail through a hemlock grove alongside the steep hill, or follow the more used road, staying to the left through a large, grassy field.

0.6   The trails rejoin and continue on a grassy jeep trail. If you follow the left option through the field, you will see a trail entering from the left just as the trails rejoin. This is where the Peaked Hill Pond Trail from West Branch Brook ride (Ride 14) ends.

0.9   At a sharp left, diverge to the right onto ATV-width singletrack. Level 3. The Peaked Hill Pond Trail (Ride 24) continues to the left.

1.0   Join an old forest road and continue to the right, traversing the hillside.

1.1   Make a quick, tight descent and cross Bagley Brook.

This crossing could be troublesome in high water. Climb the far bank, which joins an old road. Turn right and follow the road as it descends with Bagley Brook to the right. Level 2.

1.5 Cross a clearing on a rough section of trail. From here, the trail descends more rapidly.

2.1 Still descending, pass through a grassy clearing.

2.3 Pass around a wooden gate. The road improves to dirt as you begin to hear traffic on Interstate 93 and pass a cable guardrail to the right.

2.9 Follow the main dirt road past a series of logging roads on the left and right.

3.0 Pass Nordic Road which leads to Nordic Village on the right, and in 100 yards turn right onto Merrill Road. Pass under Interstate 93.

3.5 Turn right at the stop sign and go past the fire station onto paved U.S. Highway 3 (south).

5.0 Turn right onto Peaked Hill Road by the 93 Hotel. Note the Forest Service sign for the Peaked Hill Pond Trail.

5.4 Pass under Interstate 93 as the paved surface deteriorates.

5.5 Bear right past Lumber Drive.

5.6 You're back at the green Forest Service gate.

Variation: Use this ride as an alternate start to extend the Peaked Hill Pond Trail from West Branch Brook ride (Ride 14).

Thornton Gore Road

Location: 1.8 miles east of Interstate 93, exit 31, in Thornton.

Distance: 8.3-mile loop.

Time: 1 to 1.75 hours.

Tread: 3.9 miles on paved road; 2.4 miles on dirt

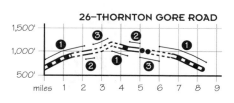

road; 0.5 mile on jeep trail; 0.3 mile on ATV-width doubletrack; 1.2 miles on ATV-width singletrack.

Aerobic level: Moderate.

Technical difficulty: 1 on paved and dirt roads; 2 on jeep trail; 3 on ATV-width singletrack and doubletrack.

Highlights: A fun loop to be incorporated with the other trails in the area (see Variations below) to make a longer ride.

Land status: Town roads; White Mountain National Forest.

Maps: WMNF Mountain Bike Map; DeLorme New Hampshire Atlas and Gazetteer, 10th edition; USGS Woodstock Quadrangle.

Access: From Interstate 93, exit 31, turn west onto Tripoli Road and go 0.1 mile, passing under the interstate to the stop sign. Go south (left) on New Hampshire 175 (Eastside Road) for 1.8 miles. Just after passing under the interstate again and as New Hampshire 175 bends sharply to the right, continue straight onto Thornton Gore Road and park in the large sandy

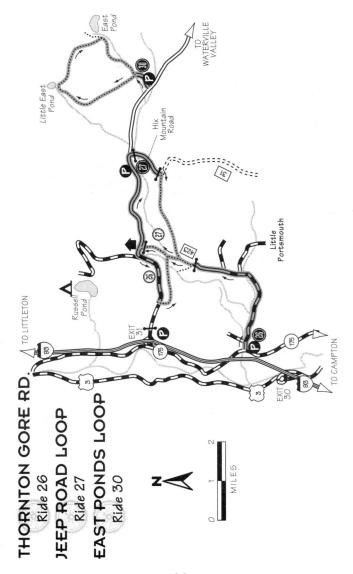

THORNTON GORE RD.
Ride 26

JEEP ROAD LOOP
Ride 27

EAST PONDS LOOP
Ride 30

East Pond

Little East Pond

TO WATERVILLE VALLEY

Hix Mountain Road

Russell Pond

TO LITTLETON

Little Portsmouth

EXIT 31

EXIT 30

TO CAMPTON

N

MILES
0   1   2

pullout on the right near this intersection. The ride begins as you leave this parking area, riding up Thornton Gore Road.

The ride

0.0 Leave the parking area and ride up Thornton Gore Road (paved).

0.1 Stay right past Sellingham Hill Road.

0.4 Follow the road across Eastman Brook.

1.0 Cross over Johnson Brook.

1.3 Bear left, climbing the hill past Johnson Brook Road and the community known as Little Portsmouth.

1.5 Bear left onto the descending dirt road, staying with Thornton Gore Road as the pavement bends right onto Dick Bradley Road. Pass several driveways.

2.0 At the bottom of a dip, begin climbing.

2.4 Pass around the Forest Service gate and bear right on the jeep trail (Forest Service Road 423) in 50 yards.

2.6 Stay right on ATV-width singletrack, past a gated road descending on the left. Keep riding as the trail becomes very grassy, passing between old stone walls and crossing several intermittent streams.

2.9 Continue straight past the intersection on the right. This is where Forest Service Road 423 turns off and where you join the Jeep Road Loop (Ride 27). Follow the sound and descend to Eastman Brook at a point where a smaller stream joins. Cross the brook on stones and regain the trail at a fire ring on the far side. This crossing could be troublesome at high water. Stay right, past a trail (Forest Service Road 426) that goes through a campsite just past the fire ring (where you will emerge on the return trip). In 10 yards, stay right again past a trail on the left leading to a campsite. Climb on wider, rocky trail.

3.1 Continue on grassy trail, past a graveyard.

3.2 Climb a more strenuous, rocky ATV-width doubletrack.

3.4 Turn left at the back side of several campsites within site of Tripoli Road.

3.5 Pass around the green Forest Service gate and turn left onto Tripoli Road (dirt), descending. (The Jeep Road Loop, Ride 27, goes right here.) Level 1.

3.6 Ride through a Forest Service gate and past the Forest Service station trailer on the left.

3.7 The road becomes paved as you pass the entrance to Russell Pond National Forest Recreation Area.

4.5 Leave White Mountain National Forest.

4.6 Turn left and descend on jeep trail around the Forest Service gate on Forest Service Road 426. Level 2.

5.1 Pass along the left edge of a log yard and continue into the woods again on ATV-width singletrack. Level 3.

5.2 Pass a trail on the right.

5.3 Cross a stream on stones.

5.5 Turn right, rejoining the trail you rode in on as you pass through a campsite. Pass the large campfire ring and cross over Eastman Brook. Ascend the steep far side bending left.

5.6 Continue straight past the intersection on the left, where you join Forest Service Road 423 and where the Jeep Road Loop (Ride 27) enters. Ride on grassy, ATV-width doubletrack over several intermittent streams.

5.9 Pass a gated road on the right and continue as the trail opens to dirt road. Bear left at the next intersection and climb to the gate. Level 1.

6.1 Pass around the Forest Service gate and descend on the dirt road.

6.3 At the bottom of a dip, begin climbing.

6.8 Bear right onto the paved road at the yield sign, staying with Thornton Gore Road past Dick Bradley Road. Pass several driveways.

7.0 Bear right, descending the hill past Johnson Brook Road and Little Portsmouth.

7.3 Cross over Johnson Brook.

7.9 Follow the road across Eastman Brook.

8.2 Stay left past Sellingham Hill Road.

8.3 Back at the parking area. Check out the swimming before you leave.

Variation: This ride is easily combined with Jeep Road Loop (Ride 27), Brown Ash Swamp (Ride 28), or Tripoli Road (Ride 34).

Jeep Road Loop

[See map page 100]

Location: 3.8 miles east of Interstate 93, exit 31, in Thornton.

Distance: 4.5-mile loop.

Time: 45 minutes to 1 hour.

Tread: 0.6 mile on jeep trail; 1.4 miles on ATV-width singletrack; 0.7 mile on ATV-width doubletrack; 1.8 miles on dirt road.

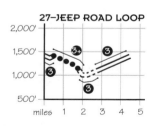

Aerobic level: Easy to moderate.

Technical difficulty: 1 on dirt road; 2 on jeep trail; 3+ on ATV-width singletrack; 3 on ATV-width doubletrack.

Highlights: A great run on ATV-width singletrack (actually an old jeep trail) and a great connector trail to lengthen the routes listed in the Variations below.

Land status: White Mountain National Forest.

Maps: WMNF Mountain Bike Map; DeLorme New Hampshire Atlas and Gazetteer, 10th edition; USGS Waterville Valley and Woodstock quadrangles.

Access: From Interstate 93, take exit 31. Turn east at the bottom of the ramp onto Tripoli Road. Follow Tripoli Road 3.8 miles (past Russell Pond Recreation Area at 1.9 miles, where the road turns to dirt) to Hix Mountain Road (Forest Service Road 31), on the right, opposite the CCC Camp road (Forest Service Road 610). Park along Tripoli Road, not blocking the gate. The ride begins as you pass around the gate on Hix Mountain Road.

The ride

0.0 Pass through the green Forest Service gate and descend Hix Mountain Road (Forest Service Road 31) on sandy jeep trail, crossing a bridge over Eastman Brook before beginning to climb. Level 2.

0.1 Continue climbing past Forest Service Road 31A on the left, then descend past several campsites on the side of the road.

0.6 At the end of the road, at a campsite, bear left around a log Forest Service gate and continue on grassy logging road for about 30 yards. Turn right on ATV-width singletrack, the old jeep trail, as the jeep trail climbs left (the Brown Ash Swamp ride, Ride 28, is to the left). The trail is rough for a short distance before climbing to a crest. Descend gradually, then more steeply over numerous water bars. Level 3+.

1.4 Cross an intermittent stream over logs and mud.

1.5 Cross three intermittent streams as you ride along old stone walls on the left and right.

1.6 Descend through a washed-out section.

1.7 Cross logs over an intermittent stream and proceed over an earth mound as you enter an old log yard overgrown with grass.

1.8 Exit the log yard at the far side on improved, wider, grassy trail. This is the top of Forest Service Road 423. Level 3.

2.1 Turn right at the junction with the improved Forest Service road, where you meet Thornton Gore Road (Ride 26). Follow the sound of cascading water and descend to Eastman Brook at a point where a smaller stream joins. Cross the brook on stones and regain the trail at a fire ring on the far side; this crossing could be troublesome at high water. Stay right, past a trail that goes to a campsite just past the fire ring, and, 10 yards beyond that, stay right again past Forest Service Road 426, where the loop closes on Thornton Gore Road (Ride 26).

2.2 Climb on wider, rocky trail

2.3 On grassy trail past a graveyard.

2.4 Climb more strenuously on rocky ATV-width doubletrack

2.6 Turn left at the back side of several campsites within site of Tripoli Road.

2.7 Pass around the green Forest Service gate and turn right onto Tripoli Road (dirt), beginning a gradual, moderately difficult climb back to the start; Thornton Gore Road (Ride 26) goes left here. Level 1.

2.8 Pass Forest Service Road 607 on the left.

3.6 Pass a logging road on the right.

3.7 Pass the 1-mile marker post on the left.

3.8 Pass gated Forest Service Road 608 on the left.

4.3 Pass Mack Brook Road on the left.

4.5 Hix Mountain Road is on the right at the beginning and end of this ride.

Variation: This ride is easily combined with Thornton Gore Road (Ride 26), Brown Ash Swamp (Ride 28), Dickey Notch Trail (Ride 29), or Tripoli Road (Ride 34).

Brown Ash Swamp

Location: 3.8 miles east of Interstate 93, exit 31, in Thornton.

Distance: 6.3-mile one way.

Time: 1.5 to 2 hours.

Tread: 3.3 miles on jeep trail; 1.2 miles on ATV-width singletrack; 1.8 miles on singletrack.

Aerobic level: Moderate.

Technical difficulty: 2 on jeep trail; 3 on ATV-width singletrack; 4 to 5 on singletrack.

Highlights: A really fun ride with challenging singletrack. This is a great ride to combine with other fine rides in the area to make a full day.

Land status: White Mountain National Forest.

Maps: WMNF Mountain Bike Map; DeLorme New Hampshire Atlas and Gazetteer, 10th edition; USGS Waterville Valley Quadrangle.

Access: From Interstate 93, take exit 31. Turn east at the bottom of the ramp onto Tripoli Road. Follow Tripoli Road 3.8 miles (past Russell Pond Recreation Area, at 1.9 miles where the

BROWN ASH SWAMP
Ride 28
DICKEY NOTCH TRAIL
Ride 29

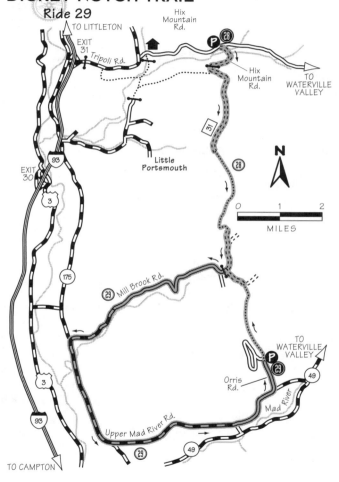

TO LITTLETON

EXIT 31

Tripoli Rd.

Hix Mountain Rd.

P 28

Hix Mountain Rd.

TO WATERVILLE VALLEY

31

28

N

0   1   2

MILES

93

EXIT 30

3

Little Portsmouth

175

29   Mill Brook Rd.

TO WATERVILLE VALLEY

P 29

Orris Rd.

49

3

Mad River

93

Upper Mad River Rd.

29   49

TO CAMPTON

road turns to dirt) to
Hix Mountain Road
(Forest Service Road
31), on the right oppo-
site the CCC Camp
road (Forest Service
Road 610). Park along

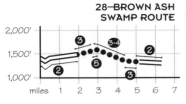

28–BROWN ASH
SWAMP ROUTE

Tripoli Road, but do not block the gate. The ride begins as you
pass around the gate on Hix Mountain Road.

The ride

0.0 Pass through the green Forest Service gate and descend
Hix Mountain Road (Forest Service Road 31) on sandy
jeep trail, crossing a bridge over Eastman Brook before
beginning to climb. Level 2.

0.1 Continue climbing past Forest Service Road 31A on the
left, and then descend past several campsites on the side
of the road.

0.6 At the end of the road, at a campsite, bear left around
a log Forest Service gate and continue on grassy logging
road. Pass the Jeep Road Loop (Ride 27) on the right as
the trail bends left and begins a long, moderate climb.

1.1 Continue climbing as the trail bends sharply to the
right.

1.4 Crest the hill and descend through an old clearcut.

2.0 The jeep trail ends. Follow ATV-width singletrack
through grass, into the woods, past a bike-trail sign.
Descend, crossing many water bars and intermittent
streams. Level 3.

2.3 Pass through a clearing. Stay left at a Y intersection as
you reenter the woods.

2.4 Cross a wooden logging bridge.

2.5	Cross through a clearing overgrown with raspberry bushes. Ouch!
2.7	Follow the beaten path to the left at this intersection. The trail becomes more washed out as you climb singletrack through rocks, roots, and mud. Level 5.
2.9	You are still climbing, but the trail becomes less difficult. Level 4 to 5.
3.4	Reach the top of a rise where the trail dips down. This is roughly where Brown Ash Swamp lies to your right in the hollow.
3.5	Crest another rise and begin descending over several whoop-de-doos.
3.8	Cross several intermittent streams.
3.9	Splash through a muddy stream.
4.0	Cross two consecutive, deep, intermittent streambeds. Continue descending as the trail becomes more grassy. Cross mud holes and water bars as the descent steepens.
4.5	Enter a grassy clearing and stay hard right, descending on a grassy, ATV-width singletrack. Level 3.
4.6	Cross Mill Brook on boulders, and descend fast trail over water bars.
5.0	Pop out onto a sand and gravel jeep trail. Level 2.
5.5	Cross over Hasselton Brook on a logging bridge and turn right at the intersection with Forest Service Road 23.
6.3	After a bit of a climb, join the Dickey Notch Trail (Ride 29), just above the Forest Service gate at mile 1.8.

Variation: This ride is easily combined with the Thornton Gore Road (Ride 26), the Jeep Road Loop (Ride 27), Dickey Notch Trail (Ride 29), or Tripoli Road (Ride 34).

Dickey Notch Trail

[See map page 107]

Location: 6.8 miles east of Interstate 93, exit 28, in Thornton.

Distance: 14.2-mile loop.

Time: 1.5 to 2 hours.

Tread: 0.8 mile on ATV-doubletrack; 1 mile on singletrack; 0.9 mile on jeep trail; 2.5 miles on dirt road; 9 miles on paved road.

Aerobic level: Moderate.

Technical difficulty: 1 on dirt and paved roads; 2 on jeep trail; 2 and 3 on ATV-width doubletrack; 3 and 4 on singletrack.

Highlights: This is fun singletrack and very beautiful riding on country roads. The section on New Hampshire 175 is the least desirable section.

Hazards: This trail can get very muddy and should be avoided on wet days to protect it from damage. Watch for traffic on New Hampshire 175.

Land status: White Mountain National Forest and town roads.

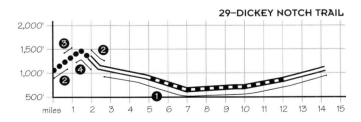

Maps: WMNF Mountain Bike Map; USGS Woodstock and Waterville Valley quadrangles (trail not shown).

Access: From Interstate 93, take exit 28. Go east at the bottom of the ramp on New Hampshire 49 toward Waterville Valley and go 5.5 miles. Turn left onto Upper Mad River Road and go 1.4 miles to Orris Road. Turn right, following the sign for Welch and Dickey and go 0.7 mile. Continue straight past Woodwinds Drive, on the left, to the dirt road into the Welch and Dickey parking area. The ride begins by the information board. There is a route map posted on this board.

The ride

0.0   Ride past the information board. Stay left on ATV-width doubletrack, following signs for the Dickey Mountain Trail. Level 2.

0.1   Continue straight, following the bike-trail sign past the hiking-trail cutoff sign. You soon pass a house on the left as you continue to ride on good trail.

0.6   Cross a series of messy water bars over rocks and mud. Level 3.

0.7   Tackle more water bars and washed-out sections of trail.

0.8   Pass a small beaver pond on the left and continue on singletrack trail.

1.0   The trail begins a moderate climb past large boulders and more technical trail. Level 4.

1.7   At the bottom of a steep downhill, follow the trail as it jogs left through a marshy section and continues to a stream crossing.

1.8   Enter a logging yard located at the end of Forest Service Road 23A in Mill Brook Valley. Return from here on the same trail, or continue to complete the loop on roads and to access the Brown Ash Swamp route (Ride 28). Continue by riding down Forest Service Road 23A on sandy and grassy jeep trail across a bridge. Level 2.

1.9 Bear left at the intersection, following the bike-trail sign.

2.6 Come to an intersection. Stay left, descending through a green Forest Service gate to complete the loop (also see Variation below).

2.7 Turn right onto Mill Brook Road (dirt), and begin a long descent, passing many driveways and side roads until you reach New Hampshire 175. Level 1.

5.2 Mill Brook Road becomes paved.

6.9 Turn south (left) onto New Hampshire 175 with a double yellow line down its middle. Watch for traffic.

7.0 Pass a graveyard on the right.

9.5 Pass the Thornton Campton Sanitary Landfill on the right and turn left at the top of the rise onto Upper Mad River Road.

10.0 Go straight past a stop sign and Mad River Road to the right.

12.2 Follow Upper Mad River Road to the left; it soon becomes dirt. Do not follow the paved road that descends.

13.4 Begin a climb past a small pond and sugar shack to the left with a fine view of Mounts Welch and Dickey. The road becomes paved.

13.5 Turn left onto Orris Road and follow the sign for Welch and Dickey mountains.

14.2 Continue straight past Woodwinds Drive, on the left, to the dirt road into the Welch and Dickey parking area.

Variation: Avoid the road riding by making this a short out-and-back ride. At 2.6 miles, this ride can be connected to the Brown Ash Swamp route by following Ride 28 in reverse.

East Ponds Loop

[Also see map page 100]

Location: 5.4 miles east of Interstate 93, exit 31, off Tripoli Road in Thornton.

Distance: 4.8 miles.

Time: 1 to 2.5 hours.

Tread: 2.3 miles on ATV-width singletrack; 2.5 miles on difficult singletrack.

30—EAST PONDS LOOP

Aerobic level: Moderate to strenuous.

Technical difficulty: 3 on ATV-width singletrack; 4, 4+, and 5 on singletrack.

Highlights: The trail begins as you follow the remains of the upper reaches of the old Woodstock and Thorton Gore logging railroad. There is great swimming from a fine gravel beach in East Pond, cleared of the normal muck by the mining of diatomaceous earth.

Hazards: The trail between the two ponds is a new trail, "virgin singletrack," and should only be attempted by expert riders or those who are willing to practice the fine art of "hike-a-bike." Be careful of small tree stumps in the trail.

Land status: White Mountain National Forest.

Maps: WMNF Mountain Bike Map; AMC Map 4 Chocorua-Waterville; DeLorme New Hampshire Atlas and Gazetteer, 10th edition; USGS Waterville Valley and Mount Osceola quadrangles (crossover trail not shown).

113

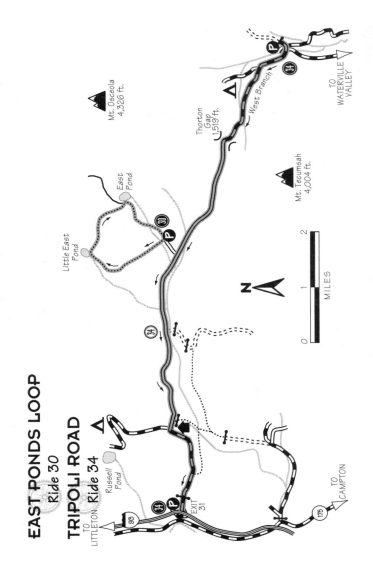

EAST PONDS LOOP
Ride 30

TRIPOLI ROAD Ride 34

Mt. Osceola
4,326 ft.

East Pond

Little East Pond

Thorton Gap
1,519 ft.

West Branch

Mt. Tecumsah
4,004 ft.

TO WATERVILLE VALLEY

N

MILES
0   1   2

Russell Pond

TO LITTLETON

93

EXIT 31

TO CAMPTON

175

114

Access: From Interstate 93, take exit 31. Turn east at the bottom of the ramp onto Tripoli Road. Follow Tripoli Road 5.2 miles (past Russell Pond Recreation Area, at 1.9 miles, where the road turns to dirt) to the East Pond Trailhead parking area on the left. Turn left and enter the gravel parking area. The ride begins at the upper end of the parking lot between the large boulders.

The ride

0.0 Begin between the boulders, riding up on the sandy, ATV-width East Pond Trail. Level 2.

0.2 Turn left at the stone cairn onto the singletrack trail and continue 50 yards to the junction with the Little East Pond Trail, which is opposite the old Tripoli Mill site (very overgrown on the right). This junction is clearly marked by a sign. Turn left onto the Little East Pond Trail (marked with yellow blazes), which follows an old, very overgrown railroad bed slightly uphill. Level 3.

0.3 Cross the small stream and in 30 yards use caution crossing a washout. You will probably have to carry over this deep washout.

0.4 Cross another small stream and several water bars.

0.6 Cross several more small streams and more water bars.

0.9 Drop down a steep bank, traverse a washed-out hillside, and cross a larger stream that is filled with large boulders; the bike will probably have to be carried over. Climb the trail up the far bank. Level 3+.

1.0 Follow the trail as it diverges sharply uphill to the right from the railroad bed, becoming singletrack. Traverse a very marshy area across many large rocks, logs, and small streams, ascending four log stairs on the far side. Level 4.

1.5 The trail climbs more steeply, with greater obstacles and encroaching underbrush increasing the technical difficulty to 4+.

1.8 There is a small, intermittent stream near a particularly root-infested section of trail that is muddy in the wet season. Traverse the boggy section on a split-log bridge and cross a small stream.

2.0 The trail eases in gradient as you come within view of shallow, tree-lined Little East Pond. Proceed to the right, following the trail sign to East Pond. Stay right again in 30 yards at a Y intersection and begin a gradual climb away from Little East Pond, traversing the hillside on narrow singletrack. This section between the ponds is a newly cut "virgin singletrack" trail through spruce and hemlock trees and is very constricted in many places. Level 5.

2.5 Descend a steep section with limited route choices.

2.7 Pass through blowdown and continue a moderate but steady descent.

2.9 Use caution and check your speed as you descend a steep blind corner to a difficult stream crossing that will most likely need to be carried over. The trail climbs the far stream bank and continues traversing the hillside, not relenting in difficulty until it gradually descends to East Pond.

3.5 Directly opposite the south end of the pond, abruptly burst into the openness of the East Pond Trail. Continue across the trail for a full view of the pond from a sandy beach. Turn right (south) and follow the East Pond Trail on an old logging road to close the loop. Level 3.

3.8 Cross several water bars.

3.9 Stream crossing.

4.1 Pick your way through watermelon-sized rocks in a washout. Level 4.

4.2 Rattle your bones as you cross logs laid out in the mud

prior to carrying across East Pond Brook on rocks or a
tree trunk.

4.6   On the right, opposite the old Tripoli Mill site, pass the
Little East Pond Trail, which you ascended on. Continue 50 yards to the junction of a more open, grassy
trail, marked by a small cairn on the left. Turn right and
follow this to the parking area. Level 3.

4.8   End of ride.

Variations: The loop can be ridden in either direction, but it
is more fun descending the East Pond Trail, which can also be
ridden beyond the pond up to Scar Ridge, but it becomes very
steep and requires technical climbing and pushing. The trail
then continues down to Kancamagus Highway.

Waterville Valley

Livermore Road

Location: 12.4 miles east of Interstate 93, exit 28, in Waterville Valley.

Distance: 4.7-mile one way.

Time: 1 hour.

Tread: 2.2 miles of dirt road and 2.5
miles of jeep trail with some obstacles and loose gravel.

Aerobic level: A moderate climb
with a fun downhill return.

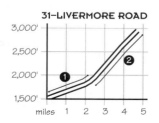

LIVERMORE ROAD
Ride 31
TIMBER CAMP TRAIL
Ride 32
GREELEY PONDS TRAIL
Ride 33

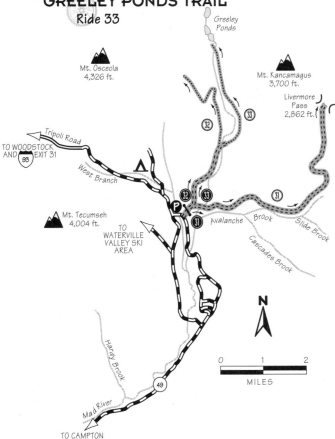

Greeley Ponds

Mt. Osceola
4,326 ft.

Mt. Kancamagus
3,700 ft.

Livermore
Pass
2,862 ft.

Tripoli Road

TO WOODSTOCK
AND **93** EXIT 31

West Branch

Mt. Tecumseh
4,004 ft.

TO
WATERVILLE
VALLEY SKI
AREA

Avalanche Brook

Slide Brook

Cascades Brook

N

Hardy Brook

Mad River

49

TO CAMPTON

0   1   2
MILES

Technical difficulty: 1 for 2.2 miles; 2 for 2.5 miles.

Highlights: A beautiful forest ride with limited mountain views. There are very nice rest or picnic spots at Boulder Path and Cascade Trail.

Land status: White Mountain National Forest.

Maps: WMNF Mountain Bike Map; DeLorme New Hampshire Atlas and Gazetteer, 10th edition; AMC Map 4 Chocorua-Waterville Valley; USGS Waterville Valley and Mount Tripyramid quadrangles.

Access: From Interstate 93, take exit 28. Go east at the bottom of the ramp on New Hampshire 49 toward Waterville Valley for 10.5 miles. Turn left on Tripoli Road, bear right in 1.2 miles at the intersection with the entrance to Waterville Valley Ski Area (do not follow the road to the ski area), and follow signs for Depot Camp and Livermore Road, an additional 0.6 mile. Turn right, cross the bridge, and turn to the left into the parking area. The trail begins at the green Forest Service gate at the entrance to the parking area. This ride shares its start with Timber Camp Trail (Ride 32) and the Greeley Ponds Trail (Ride 33).

The ride

0.0 Ride around the steel gate and down Livermore Road.

0.3 Pass through a clearing; as you enter the woods on the far side, continue past the cutoff for the Greeley Ponds Trail (Ride 33).

0.5 Cross a bridge over the Mad River and continue up the rise past Boulder Path. Boulder Path is a nice spot to rest or picnic.

0.9 Continue past Kettle Path on the left.

1.1 Climb gradually through a clearing with mountain views to the right.

1.8 Continue past the Norway Rapids Trail, which descends to the right. Norway Rapids are 0.1 mile down this trail and worth a look.

2.2 Follow the sign for the Livermore Trail, bearing to the left before the bridge. The trail narrows to a jeep trail here and begins to climb more gradually. Level 2. (Note: If you continue straight across this bridge, you enter Snows Mountain and the Waterville Valley permit trail system. To do this a trail pass is required.)

2.6 Continue left past the South Slide Tripyramid Trail.

3.2 Pass through the Avalanche Camp clearing (an old logging camp) as the trail steepens slightly and becomes more grassy with some washouts and rocks.

3.7 Follow the trail up and to the left around a hairpin turn as you pass the North Slide Tripyramid Trail on the right.

3.9 Pass the Scaur Ridge Trail on the right and continue over three water bars before a short, steep climb.

4.6 The trail flattens considerably.

4.7 You're at a vehicle turnaround on the left and the top of Livermore Pass (2,862 feet), a col between Mounts Tripyramid and Kancamagus. This is the turnaround point of this ride.

Variations: Continue over the pass and descend the trail, which becomes narrower and more technical and emerges on Kancamagus Highway (New Hampshire 112). You can also link this ride to the Waterville Valley trail system, but you must first obtain a trail pass, available at the Waterville Valley Base Camp Adventure Center (see Appendix A).

Timber Camp Trail

[See map page 118]

Location: 12.4 miles east of Interstate 93, exit 28, in Waterville Valley.

Distance: 3-mile one way.

Time: 30 minutes to 1 hour.

Tread: 1.4 miles on dirt road; 0.8 mile on ATV-width singletrack; 0.8 mile on singletrack.

Aerobic level: Strenuous all the way up.

Technical difficulty: 1+ but climbing; 3+ after switchback.

Highlights: Tune up your brakes for this excellent descent following a challenging, near-continuous climb. Excellent views of Mount Kancamagus, Mount Tripyramid, and the Painted Cliffs are your reward for the pain you will suffer.

Land status: White Mountain National Forest.

Maps: WMNF Mountain Bike Map; AMC Map 4 Chocorua-Waterville Valley; DeLorme New Hampshire Atlas and Gazetteer, 10th edition; USGS Waterville Valley Quadrangle.

Access: From Interstate 93, take exit 28. Go east at the bottom of the ramp onto New Hampshire 49 toward Waterville Valley for 10.5 miles. Turn left on Tripoli Road, bear right in 1.2 miles at the intersection with the entrance to Waterville Valley Ski Area (do not follow the road to the ski area), and follow signs for Depot Camp and Livermore Road, an additional 0.6 mile. Turn right, cross the bridge, and turn to the left into the parking area. The trail begins at the green Forest Service gate where you enter the parking area. The beginning of this ride is the same as for Livermore Road (Ride 31) and the Greeley Ponds Trail (Ride 33).

The ride

0.0   Ride around the steel Forest Service gate and down Livermore Road.

0.3   Pass through a clearing and, on the far side, turn left at the sign indicating the beginning of the Greeley Ponds Trail. This old logging road has some rough sections but is quite rideable. Level 1+.

1.0   Continue straight past the Scaur Trail on the right.

1.3   Continue straight past the Goodrich Rock Trail on the left.

1.4   At the Y intersection, stay left, leave the Greeley Ponds Trail and begin climbing. The trail becomes ATV-width singletrack and climbs, continuously traversing the south side of Mount Osceola. The trail continues upward and crosses many water bars.

1.5   Dip down to an intermittent stream and climb the loose, sandy surface on the other side.

1.9   Stream crossing.

2.1   Find your granny gear, because you'll soon be needing them. At the Y intersection, stay left, and climb more steeply, following the sign for High Camp. The right-hand option, signposted "Greeley Brook," dead ends.

2.2   Switch back to the left and follow the trail as it wraps around to the right and gets steeper and more difficult. Level 3+.

2.5   Climb a water bar. The trail jogs left, still climbing, around a viewpoint overlooking the mountains and the surrounding Waterville Valley.

2.6   Climb through a sandy section of trail.

2.7 The trail turns left. Pause, if you haven't already, to enjoy the view of Mount Tripyramid.

2.8 The trail levels briefly before dropping over a water bar and resumes climbing through a grassy and mossy section.

2.9 Stream crossing.

3.0 Enter a rocky clearing with the Painted Cliffs above. You made it! Check out the view and catch your breath before beginning the descent. Check your speed and don't run down any hikers.

Greeley Ponds Trail
[See map page 118]

Location: 12.4 miles east of Interstate 93, exit 28, in Waterville Valley.

Distance: 3.2-mile one way.

Time: 1 to 1.5 hours.

Tread: 1.7 miles on dirt road; 1.3 miles on ATV-width double- and singletrack; 0.2 mile on singletrack.

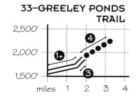

Aerobic level: Moderate.

Technical difficulty: 1+ on dirt-road sections; 3 and 4 near top on ATV-width doubletrack and singletrack.

Highlights: A challenging ride with beautiful views of the upper Mad River and the first Greeley Pond. Opportunities exist to fish and see beaver and other wildlife.

Land status: White Mountain National Forest.

Maps: WMNF Mountain Bike Map; AMC Map 4 Chocorua-Waterville Valley; DeLorme New Hampshire Atlas and Gazetteer, 10th edition; USGS Waterville Valley, Mount Osceola, and Mount Tripyramid quadrangles.

Access: From Interstate 93, take exit 28. Go east at the bottom of the ramp onto New Hampshire 49 toward Waterville Valley for 10.5 miles. Turn left on Tripoli Road, bear right in 1.2 miles at the intersection with the entrance to Waterville Valley Ski Area (do not follow the road to the ski area), and follow signs for Depot Camp and Livermore Road, an additional 0.6 mile. Turn right, cross the bridge, and turn to the left into the parking area. The trail begins at the green Forest Service gate as you enter the parking area. The beginning of this ride is the same as for the Livermore Road ride (Ride 31) and the Timber Camp Trail (Ride 32).

The ride

0.0 Ride around the steel gate on Livermore Road.

0.3 Pass through a clearing. On the far side, turn left at the sign indicating the beginning of the Greeley Ponds Trail. This old logging road has some rough sections but is quite rideable. Level 1+.

1.0 Continue straight past the Scaur Trail on the right.

1.3 Continue straight past the Goodrich Rock Trail on the left.

1.4 Stay right at the Y, and cross over the Mad River on a wooden bridge (Knight's Bridge).

1.6 Continue past the Flume Trail on the right and climb over a bouldery section to the right. The trail becomes more technical, challenging you with rocks and roots before crossing back over the Mad River on a wooden bridge. Level 3.

1.7 Trail narrows to ATV-width singletrack. Level 4.

1.8 Drop down to face the challenge of an often-muddy hole or ride the log walkway.

1.9	Cross a small wooden bridge.
2.2	Cross a small wooden bridge. In a slightly easier section of trail hop over three water bars.
2.6	Pass a boulder on the right and cross a bridge.
2.6	Cross a small wooden bridge.
2.7	Climb up a series of log steps.
2.8	Cross a small wooden bridge.
3.0	Continue following the sign for the Greeley Ponds Trail past a trail that descends to the left; then climb to the right over loose dirt, rock, and roots. The trail is singletrack. Level 4.
3.1	Crest the rise and drop down to the left onto a wooden bridge with railings.
3.2	Stop (!) or you're going to ride straight into the first Greeley Pond.

Tripoli Road
[See map page 114]

Location: 12.4 miles east of Interstate 93, exit 28, in Waterville Valley.

Distance: 9.4-mile one way.

Time: 1 to 2 hours.

Tread: 4.5 miles on paved road; 4.9 miles on dirt road.

Aerobic level: Easy to moderate.

Technical difficulty: 1 on paved and dirt roads.

Highlights: This ride follows the very scenic and narrow Tripoli Road, named for the diatomaceous earth mined from East Pond (see Ride 30), between Waterville Valley and Woodstock. The road can be ridden in either direction, but a ride from Waterville climbs moderately on a paved surface to Thornton Gap (1,519 feet) before making a longer descent on a dirt surface to Woodstock. A second vehicle can be left at the end of the ride, 0.3 mile east of Interstate 93, exit 31, on Tripoli Road.

Hazards: Be cautious of vehicular traffic along this popular scenic drive, especially during summer and fall foliage season.

Land status: White Mountain National Forest.

Maps: WMNF Mountain Bike Map; DeLorme New Hampshire Atlas and Gazetteer, 10th edition; AMC Map 4 Chocorua-Waterville; USGS Woodstock and Waterville Valley quadrangles.

Access: From Interstate 93, take exit 28. Go east at the bottom of the ramp, onto New Hampshire 49, toward Waterville Valley for 10.5 miles. Turn left on Tripoli Road, bear right in 1.2 miles at the intersection with the entrance to Waterville Valley Ski Area (do not follow the road to the ski area), and follow signs for Depot Camp and Livermore Road, an additional 0.6 mile. Turn right, cross the bridge, and turn to the left into the parking area. The trail begins at the green Forest Service gate as you enter the parking area.

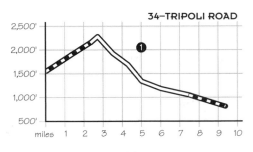

The ride

0.0   Begin the ride as you leave the entrance to the parking area. Stay to the right past the green Forest Service gate on your left. Cross the West Branch of the Mad River on the road bridge and turn right onto Tripoli Road. Follow the sign to Russell Pond Campground. Begin the long, moderate climb on the paved road.

0.3   Pass through the green Forest Service gate and go past the 7-mile marker post as you cross Tecumseh Brook.

0.4   Continue on the paved surface past Osceola Vista Campground on the right.

1.3   Pass the 6-mile marker post as you continue up the road through the canopy of trees with the soothing sound of the West Branch of the Mad River accompanying you from the right.

1.6   Cross the West Branch on a bridge. You will pass a sign indicating that car parking is allowed only on the south side of the road.

2.3   Pass the 5-mile marker post.

2.5   Cross the Waterville-Livermore town line marked by a post on the right.

2.7   Climb more steeply for 0.1 mile.

2.8   Crest the hill at Thornton Gap (2,318 feet) as the road turns to dirt and begins the big descent to Woodstock. Go through a green Forest Service gate and pass the Mount Osceola Trailhead on the right.

3.3   Reach the 4-mile marker post.

3.7   Are you suffering from clamper cramps yet?

3.8   Cross a small bridge and pass Beaver Pond Road on the right.

4.0   Continue descending past the Mount Tecumseh Trailhead on the left.

4.3   Pass the East Pond Trailhead on the right (where East Ponds Loop, Ride 30, begins).

4.4   Reach the 3-mile marker post and a logging road on the right.

5.4	Reach the 2-mile marker post.
5.8	Pass Hix Mountain Road, descending back to the left, (see Jeep Road Loop, Ride 27, and Brown Ash Swamp, Ride 28) and the CCC camp road to the right.
5.9	Mack Brook Road leaves to the right.
6.4	Pass a Forest Service road on the right and the 1-mile marker post
7.4	Pass a Forest Service road on the right.
7.6	Ride through a Forest Service gate and past the Forest Service station trailer on the left.
7.7	The road becomes paved as you pass the entrance to Russell Pond National Forest Recreation Area.
8.6	Leave White Mountain National Forest.
9.4	Pass through a steel gate; end of ride.

Variation: The East Ponds Loop (Ride 30) can be added for a very challenging side trip. Starts at mile 9.4.

Plymouth

Le Tour de Plymouth

Location: 0.6 mile west of Interstate 93, exit 25, in Plymouth.

Distance: 5.2-mile loop.

Time: 30 minutes to 1 hour.

Tread: 3.0 miles on paved road; 0.2 mile on dirt road; 0.2 mile on jeep trail; 0.4 mile on ATV-width doubletrack; 1.4 miles on singletrack.

Aerobic level: Moderate.

Technical difficulty: 1 on
paved roads; 2 on ATV-width
doubletrack and jeep trail; 3 on
singletrack.

Highlights: A loop giving you
a look at the parks, neighbor-
hoods, and Main Street of Plymouth. Stop in at any of the
delis or pubs to refuel as you
ride down Main Street.

Land status: Private land, town land and roads.

Maps: DeLorme New Hampshire Atlas and Gazetteer, 10th edition (may be helpful); USGS Plymouth Quadrangle.

Access: From Interstate 93, exit 25, go 0.5 mile west on New
Hampshire 175A. Just across the bridge (before the stop sign and
blinking red light) turn left onto Green Street and go 0.1 mile, past
the district court building to the municipal parking lot and find
a parking space. The ride begins in front of the district court
building.

The ride

0.0 Begin in front of the district court building. Return
north on Green Street.
0.1 At the stop sign, turn left onto New Hampshire 175A
west and go across the railroad tracks to the stop sign
under the red blinking light. Turn right onto U.S. Highway 3 north (Main Street).
0.4 Following signs for the Heritage Trail, turn left onto
Toby Road.
0.5 At the top of the first rise, turn right onto Armory Road.
0.6 Stay to the right, crossing the armory parking lot to the
northeast corner.

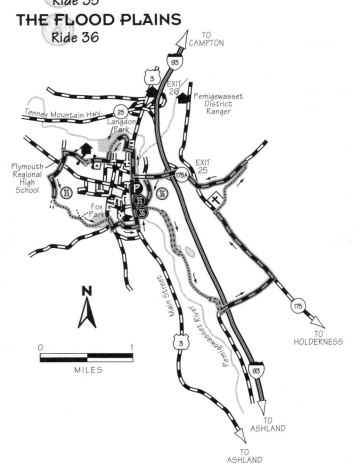

LE TOUR DE PLYMOUTH
Ride 35
THE FLOOD PLAINS
Ride 36

TO
CAMPTON

93

3

EXIT
26

Pemigewasset
District
Ranger

Tenney Mountain Hwy.

25

Langdon
Park

Plymouth
Regional
High
School

35

175A

EXIT
25

36

Fox
Park

P
35

36

N

0   1

MILES

Main Street

Pemigewasset River

3

175

TO
HOLDERNESS

93

TO
ASHLAND

TO
ASHLAND

0.7 Follow a singletrack trail cutting through the row of trees. As you enter the field, check out the commemorative plaque on the boulder to the right on the edge of U.S. Highway 3. The plaque commemorates the original village site of the Pemigewasset Indians. The trail continues to the left across the field until you join another singletrack. Go right, continuing to follow the edge of the field until you meet a jeep trail that soon turns to sandy ATV-width doubletrack and drops left into the woods of Langdon Park. Level 2.

1.0 Follow the trail along the Baker River and across a wooden bridge to a makeshift BMX park. Follow the main trail through the park to a clearing, or spend some time on the many dirt jumps and other fun obstacles available here for hurting yourself and your bike.

1.1 Turn left, leaving the Heritage Trail in the grass clearing. Ride away from the beach (a good swimming hole with a sandy beach on the Baker River) and follow a wide, grassy singletrack into the woods.

1.3 As you crest a rise, continue past a trail on the right. The trail opens up, becoming grassy again. Pass two manhole covers on the right.

1.4 Join a gravel road, staying left. Ride around the chain-link gate to the left, past several houses, and onto Langdon Park Road (paved). Level 1.

1.6 Turn right at the stop sign onto Merrill Street.

1.7 Continue to the right past a stop sign.

1.9 Ride around the chain, onto the access road, past the football field, and up and around the high school building.

2.0 Stay right through the parking lot as it passes in front of the building. Follow the yellow curb.

2.2 Pass by Plymouth Elementary School and follow the driveway as it climbs to the left.

2.4 Go past the stop sign under the blinking light and continue directly across Highland Street onto Reservoir Road.

2.6	Turn left onto Bink's Hill Road.
2.7	Bink's Hill Road becomes dirt.
2.9	Pass the last house on Bink's Hill Road and continue into the woods on the jeep trail. Climb moderately. Level 2.
3.0	Stay left at the Y.
3.1	Follow the singletrack trail, climbing sharply to the left. Level 3.
3.2	The singletrack begins a very fun descent on smooth dirt trail through very navigable rock obstacles.
3.5	Bend sharply right through a swampy section. Climb out the far side on smooth trail under pine trees.
3.7	Pass several large boulders on the left and cross through an opening in a stone wall. Descend to a mud hole crossed on wooden planks.
3.9	Take the right-hand descending trail at a four-way junction with a large pine tree in the center.
4.0	Cross an intermittent streambed.
4.1	Emerge into Fox Park. Cross through the picnic area toward the buildings and descend the gravel access road around the chain gate to the parking area.
4.2	Turn right onto Langdon Street (paved) and climb to the intersection. Level 1.
4.3	Turn left onto Warren Street, unmarked, at the four-way intersection.
4.5	Turn left onto Main Street (U.S. Highway 3 north). Ride past the many shops, pubs, and delis: perfect refueling opportunities.
4.8	Pass Plymouth's Town Common.
5.0	Turn right onto New Hampshire 175A east (Bridge Street) under the blinking light.
5.1	Just across the railroad tracks, turn right onto Green Street.
5.2	You are back in front of the Plymouth district court building.

Variations: There are many possible variations on the many trails through Langdon Park. Explore and create your own. This ride can also be joined to the Flood Plains ride (Ride 36).

The Flood Plains
[See map page 130]

Location: 0.6 mile west of Interstate 93, exit 25, in Plymouth.

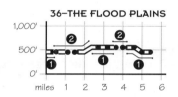

Distance: 5.4-mile loop.

Time: 45 minutes to 1 hour.

Tread: 3.3 miles on paved road; 0.7 mile on jeep trail; 1.4 miles on singletrack.

Aerobic level: Easy, with one climb on sandy jeep trail.

Technical difficulty: 1 on paved roads; 2 on jeep trail and singletrack.

Highlights: You get one of the best views around of Plymouth nestled in the forested valley. You also ride through a beautiful graveyard.

Hazards: Watch for traffic on New Hampshire 175 and U.S. Highway 3.

Land status: Private and town roads. Please be respectful of the trails—as with all others—since many of them are maintained and monitored by local snowmobile clubs.

Maps: DeLorme New Hampshire Atlas and Gazetteer, 10th edition (may be helpful); USGS Plymouth and Ashland quadrangles.

Access: From Interstate 93, exit 25, go 0.5 mile west on New Hampshire 175A. Just across the bridge (before the stop sign and blinking red light) turn left onto Green Street and go 0.1 mile past the district court building to the municipal parking lot and find a parking space. The ride begins in front of the district court building.

The ride

0.0 Begin in front of the district court building. Ride north on Green Street.

0.1 At the stop sign, turn right onto New Hampshire 175A, crossing the bridge.

0.2 Just past the bridge, turn right onto South River Street and ride to its end.

0.5 Continue past the end of South River Street into the woods on singletrack. Follow the trail as it bends left. Level 2.

0.7 Turn right as the singletrack ends at a sandy jeep trail.

0.8 Continue past a trail on the left into a small, grassy field.

1.0 Follow the trail to the left around the pond as you leave the clearing. In 25 yards, cross a snowmobile bridge to the right, passing through a V notch in the steel gate. Continue on lush singletrack.

1.2 Follow the singletrack as it heads out across a series of hay fields.

1.4 Continue into the second hay field, staying to the right edge.

1.8 Follow the trail as it becomes jeep trail heading across the field to the left.

2.0 Follow the jeep trail, exiting into the bush and climbing on sand and gravel.

2.2 At the top of the hill, before crossing to the left of the cable gate, take a side trip about a hundred yards down the trail on the right to the far end of the field for a great view of Plymouth. To continue, pass the cable to the left and turn left onto North Ashland Road (paved), passing over Interstate 93. Level 1.

2.9 Turn left at the stop sign onto New Hampshire 175 north. Use caution: this is a busy road.

3.6 After the big dip in the road, turn right into the graveyard. Pass through the iron gate and follow Central Avenue through the center of this beautiful burial ground, passing a small fountain.

3.7 At the end of Central Avenue, turn right. In about 30 yards, at the graveyard's corner, exit left around a wooden fence on singletrack. Level 2.

3.9 Continue past a trail on the left.

4.0 Continue past a trail on the right.

4.1 Emerge from the woods and turn left onto paved Mount Prospect Road. Level 1.

4.8 Turn right opposite Holderness School at a stop sign onto New Hampshire 175. Immediately, stay left onto New Hampshire 175A west, following the sign for Interstate 93.

4.9 Pass under Interstate 93.

5.3 Cross over the bridge and turn left onto Green Street.

5.4 Finish in front of the district court building.

Variation: Combine this ride with Le Tour de Plymouth (Ride 35).

Plymouth Mountain Loop

Location: 8.1 miles west of Interstate 93, exit 25, in Plymouth.

Distance: 12.3-mile loop.

Time: 1.5 to 3 hours.

Tread: 6.0 miles on jeep trail; 4.1 miles on dirt road; 2.2 miles on paved road.

Aerobic level: Moderate to strenuous. The biggest climbs are on the dirt and paved roads.

Technical difficulty: 2, 3, 3-, and 4 on jeep trail; 2 on dirt road; 1 on paved road.

Highlights: The jeep-trail portion of this ride is absolutely beautiful. You ride past stone walls, get great lake and mountain views, and it's mostly downhill. The ride to close the loop is a hump over several long climbs but is also beautiful and passes several classic New Hampshire farms.

Land status: Private lands and town roads.

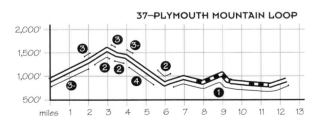

PLYMOUTH MOUNTAIN LOOP
Ride 37
GROTON HOLLOW
Ride 38

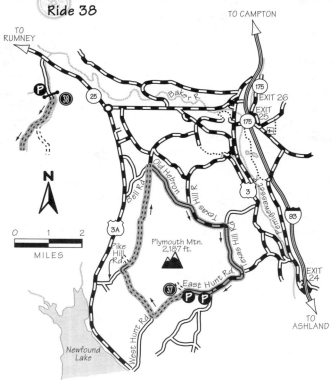

Maps: DeLorme New Hampshire Atlas and Gazetteer, 10th edition; USGS Ashland, Newfound, Rumney, and Plymouth quadrangles.

Access: From Interstate 93, exit 25, go 0.6 mile west on New Hampshire 175A. At the stop sign and blinking light, turn south (left) onto U.S. Highway 3 (Main Street) and go 0.5 mile around the town center to the south end of town. Turn right onto Warren Street (as you are leaving town) and follow it 0.2 mile to a four-way intersection. Go straight through the intersection onto Texas Hill Road for 5 miles, bearing left at the "Big Rock" (2.1 miles) and right at Cummings Hill Road (3.5 miles) where the road becomes dirt. Turn right onto Dick Brown Road (paved) and go 1.1 miles past where the road turns to dirt (0.9 mile). Turn right onto Hunt Road East. Park at this intersection if your vehicle has poor clearance. Otherwise, go 0.7 mile, past a house on the right and several driveways, bearing right at 0.6 mile. Park on the side of the road where a logging road leaves to the right, blocked by large boulders, and Hunt Road disappears into the woods, becoming narrow and grassy. The ride begins as you follow Hunt Road into the woods.

The ride

0.0 Follow Old Hunt Road to the left as it narrows to jeep path and enters the forest.

0.1 Cross a small stream and begin a moderate climb. In 40 yards cross a bridge. Level 3-.

0.3 Pass a hunting camp back in the woods to the left.

0.6 From the top of a rise, descend briefly to a washed-out section of trail.

0.9 Pass a log landing on the left as you continue to descend.

1.0 Cross a small wooden bridge and climb gradually.

1.3 Emerge from the woods at a red house with white trim

atop a rise with a commanding view of Newfound Lake. Turn right just before the house as Hunt Road becomes driveable again. Head for an old road, entering the woods across the grass.

1.7 Surmount ledge outcrop. Level 3.

1.8 Pass a log landing on the right as the trail becomes grassy.

1.9 Cross a tiny stream and attack the grapefruit-sized rocks on the far side. From here the trail climbs steeply up a beautiful grassy surface. Level 2.

2.1 Pass a trail leaving to the left and continue to the top of the hill. Begin a really sweet downhill run.

2.3 Pass a trail to the right, and continue gliding through a canopy of trees, down the grassy, centered trail lined by a stone wall.

2.8 Catch a great view of Newfound Lake through a break in the trees opposite a trail to the right going to a cabin. The descent steepens and you cross several water bars.

3.1 Check your speed as you cross a washed-out section of trail. Level 3.

3.2 Turn right at Pike Hill Road, opposite a house, and ride on a much-improved dirt road. Level 2.

3.4 Pass a log landing on the right as the road becomes grassy jeep trail and you enter the woods on a beautiful trail.

3.8 Begin a descent on a grassy, mossy trail.

4.0 Use caution, as the trail is washed out. Level 3-.

4.2 Pass through a clearing that is often muddy.

4.5 Pass an overgrown logging road on the right. Stay on your toes through some technical sections, crossing wet, mossy rocks. Level 4.

4.8 The trail becomes less technical for a while as you ride on grassy trail.

4.9 Pass Pike Hill Cottage on the right.

5.2 Pass a snowmobile trail on the right and descend into a badly washed-out trail.

5.5 Continue past a trail on the right and over difficult trail and a culvert pipe.

5.6 Cross a culvert pipe and enter a log landing. Pass through the landing on improved trail. Level 2.

6.2 Exit the woods past a chain gate at the intersection of Old Hebron Road and Bell Road. Turn right, climbing up Old Hebron Road (dirt). Level 1.

6.6 Your reward for your climb is a fine view of the valley below.

6.7 Begin descending, soon passing two beautiful farms, the first with a red barn on the left.

7.3 Descend more steeply on a short paved section of road.

7.8 Come to the locally infamous "Big Rock" at the intersection where Old Hebron Road ends at Texas Hill Road. Make sure to pay homage to this well-known local landmark as you respectfully pass it. Stay to the right, riding onto Texas Hill Road (paved).

8.3 Begin a long, strenuous climb.

8.8 Breathe easy as you crest the hill and begin a descent, a payoff for the preceding climb.

9.1 Stay right onto dirt surface as Cummings Hill Road intersects from the left. Continue mostly downhill with a few climbs.

10.6 Turn right onto Dick Brown Road (paved) and begin a long climb again.

11.5 The road turns to dirt.

11.7 Turn right onto Hunt Road East and steeply ascend the dirt road.

12.0 Continue straight past a house and a driveway marked with a "No Trespassing" sign on the right. The dirt road becomes rougher here as you pass several logging roads.

12.2 Bear right.

12.3 Find yourself happily back at the start of your ride.

Groton Hollow

[See map page 137]

Location: 7.3 miles west of Interstate 93, exit 26, in Rumney.

Distance: 2.3-mile one way.

Time: 40 minutes to 1 hour.

Tread: All on good jeep trail.

Aerobic level: Moderate, with a steep climb for the first 0.8 mile or so.

38–GROTON HOLLOW

Technical difficulty: 2 on jeep trail.

Highlights: A technically easy ride with an excellent return ride downhill.

Land status: Private.

Maps: DeLorme New Hampshire Atlas and Gazetteer, 10th edition; USGS Rumney Quadrangle.

Access: From Interstate 93, exit 26, go west on New Hampshire 25 (Tenney Mountain Highway) for 4 miles to the rotary. Take the first right, following New Hampshire 25 for 2.2 miles, and turn left onto Groton Hollow Road. Follow this road 1.1 miles past where it turns to dirt (0.2 mile), bearing left at a Y intersection to its end, 100 yards farther. Park at the turnaround. The ride begins at the gate just past the last house on the road.

The ride

0.0   Ride past the steel gate up the sandy jeep trail. Stay right past a logging road and bridge on the left.

0.2   The climb becomes more strenuous.

0.8   Follow the main road past a logging road and bridge, on the left, as the climb eases.

1.2   The road bends right past a log landing.

1.3   Cross the intersection with New Hampshire Snowmobile Corridor 11 and proceed to a Y intersection 30 yards farther. Stay to the right.

1.7   Pass an old sand pit on the left.

2.0   Cross a stream on a culvert, staying right through the log landing.

2.1   Cross back over the stream on another culvert.

2.3   The ride ends at this large log landing. There are several skidder trails you could explore from here. If you venture on, watch out for derailleur- and spoke-breaking sticks.

39

Plymouth-Rumney RR Grade

[See map page 55]

Location: 1.4 miles west of Interstate 93, exit 26 (Tenney Mountain Highway), in Plymouth.

Distance: 3.9-mile one way.

Time: 30 minutes to 1 hour.

Tread: 0.6 mile on singletrack; 3.0 miles on jeep trail on sand and cinder; 0.3 mile on paved road.

39—PLYMOUTH-
RUMNEY RR GRADE

Aerobic level: Easy.

Technical difficulty: 1 on jeep trail and paved road; 2 on singletrack.

Highlights: This is the perfect ride for the person who wants a short cruise with no hills or technical terrain. The ride follows a straight line on the old Boston and Main railroad grade between Plymouth and Rumney.

Land status: Private.

Maps: DeLorme New Hampshire Atlas and Gazetteer, 10th edition; USGS Rumney and Plymouth quadrangles.

Access: From Interstate 93, exit 26, go west 0.1 mile on New Hampshire 25 (Tenney Mountain Highway), staying right immediately after passing under the last overpass. Take the first exit ramp, following the signs for U.S. Highway 3. At the top of the ramp, turn left onto U.S. Highway 3 north and immediately left again, opposite McDonald's, onto Fairgrounds Road. Go 1.3 miles and turn left onto Cooksville Road (opposite Beech Hill Road on the right). Park along Cooksville Road so as not to obstruct traffic. The ride begins 0.1 mile down Cooksville Road from the intersection with Fairgrounds Road on the singletrack descending west (right) under the powerlines.

The ride

0.0   Ride west, descending on sandy singletrack, from Cooksville Road to the railroad grade under the powerline. Level 2.

0.2   Cross a gravel driveway.

0.5   Cross behind a power substation on grassy trail and cross a gravel driveway. The trail becomes jeep trail. Level 1.

0.8   Cross a driveway.

1.7   Turn left and follow Fairgrounds Road west on pavement.

1.9   Turn right onto Loon Lake Road.

2.0   Turn left onto a dirt driveway, following the old railroad grade under the powerlines again.

2.4   As the driveway bends right, follow a singletrack slightly left over an earth berm, continuing under the powerlines. Level 2.

2.5   Ride over another earth berm and rejoin the railroad grade on jeep trail. Level 1.

2.9   Ride over an earth berm.

3.0   Ride over an earth berm.

3.2   Cross a dirt driveway.

3.9 Come to Quincy Road (paved). Turn around here or return on paved roads (see Variations below). The railroad grade is still rideable from here for some distance but crosses lands that are gated and becomes more difficult to follow.

Variations: Return on paved roads by turning left onto Quincy Road and riding 1.7 miles. Turn left onto Fairgrounds Road at the Y, riding 2.3 miles (crossing the railroad grade in 0.5 mile) to Cooksville Road and the start of the ride. This ride can also be combined with the East Rumney–Campton Bog Road ride (Ride 12).

Warren

Warren–East Haverhill RR Grade

Location: 19.8 miles west of Interstate 93, exit 26, in Warren.

Distance: 6.2-mile one way.

Time: 1 to 1.75 hours for longest option one way.

Tread: 6.2 miles on jeep trail (smooth old railroad bed); if Variation 2 is ridden, additional 3.6 miles on ATV-width doubletrack.

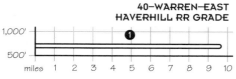

40–WARREN–EAST HAVERHILL RR GRADE

WARREN-EAST HAVERHILL RR GRADE
Ride 40
MEADER (WACHIPAUKA) POND
Ride 41

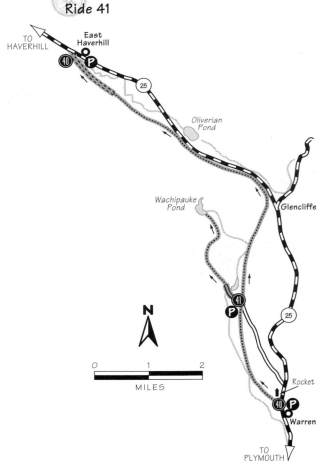

TO
HAVERHILL

East
Haverhill

40 P

25

Oliverian
Pond

Wachipauke
Pond

Glencliffe

N

41 P

25

0   1   2
MILES

Rocket

40 P

Warren

TO
PLYMOUTH

Aerobic level: Easy; easy to moderate if Variation 2 is chosen.

Technical difficulty: 1 on railroad bed and dirt roads; 2+ on ATV-width doubletrack.

Highlights: A very pleasant, easy ride that follows the old Boston and Maine railroad grade. There is good birding potential, particularly at the East Haverhill end as you enter a preserve.

Hazards: Be careful of traffic on New Hampshire 25. Also be alert for ATV traffic on the trail.

Land status: White Mountain National Forest; town roads; private land.

Maps: WMNF Mountain Bike Map; USGS Warren and East Haverhill quadrangles.

Access: From Interstate 93, take exit 26, New Hampshire 25 (Tenney Mountain Highway) west and go 4 miles to the rotary. Take the first right, following New Hampshire 25 for 15.8 miles to the town of Warren, where you will see the rocket next to the fire station. Park near the rocket. If you wish to make this a one-way ride, position a vehicle at the ball park in East Haverhill (continue on New Hampshire 25 for 9.3 miles to the ballpark on the left just before Olivarian Valley Campground Wildlife Preserve). The ride begins from the rocket and goes north along the railroad grade; look for the "Jesse Bushaw Memorial Trail" sign.

The ride

0.0 Begin the ride at the rocket by the information board. If your curiosity has been piqued by the rocket—which is actually a Jupiter C Satellite Launch Vehicle—all your informational needs concerning this town centerpiece can be fulfilled by reading the reverse side of the information board. Ride north along the wide, smooth, gravel railroad grade; look for the "Jesse Bushaw Memorial Trail" sign on the right.

0.1   Enter the woods.

0.3   Pass a logging road on the right, following the main railroad grade. Be cautious of ATV riders who may be darting onto the trail from side trails along the next mile.

2.5   Cross a dirt road (Weeks Crossing) with utility lines overhead. To make a shorter loop back to the rocket (Variation 1), you can turn right here; to the left, you can access the Meader (Wachipauka) Pond ride (Ride 41).

3.4   Stay to the right on the main railroad grade, past a park bench and a trail on the left.

3.5   Pass a small pond on the left.

3.7   If you like, rest on the park bench to the left at Black Brook Bog Natural Area. The ride continues straight, following along the railroad grade.

4.0   Pass a spring flowing from a black pipe on the left as you ride through a deep, dark cut in the hill.

4.5   Follow the main trail as it bends around to make a small stream crossing and emerge on a dirt road under a utility line. This is Station Road in Glencliff. Zigzag to the left and regain the railroad bed in 30 yards, just before entering the driveway to a home.

4.9   Cross the Appalachian Trail (there's a parking area on the roadside to the right; note that biking is not allowed on the Appalachian Trail). Continue as New Hampshire 25 follows within sight on the right for a while.

5.3   Cross a driveway.

5.9   Pass through a grassy clearing.

6.2   Turn around and return on the same route, or continue (see Variations 2 and 3).

Variation 1:

2.5   Loop back to the rocket by turning right at Weeks

Crossing. Follow the dirt road, gradually climbing past a "Children Playing" sign.

3.7 Stay right at the intersection with Swain Hill Road, past another "Children Playing" sign, onto the paved surface.

4.6 Begin a fast and fun descent, passing a graveyard.

4.9 Bear right at the bottom of the hill by the stop sign and ride east on New Hampshire 25.

5.5 Stay right in front of the fire station and return to the rocket.

Variation 2:

6.2 The trail becomes ATV-width doubletrack and more difficult for the next 0.7 mile as the old railroad bed actually follows New Hampshire 25. Follow the trail as it makes a short steep climb to the left. Level 2+.

6.3 Drop into a hollow and cross a snowmobile bridge at the bottom and a second bridge as you ascend the far side.

6.5 Cross another snowmobile bridge.

6.7 Descend abruptly, crossing several more snowmobile bridges. Make one final ascent on a rocky section of trail.

6.9 Zip down a hill and stay left as you regain the railroad grade and cross a small wooden bridge. Level 1.

7.4 Pass a water-filled quarry on the left.

8.3 Cross a small bridge and proceed through a clearing with a trail ascending to the left.

8.5 Carry around five concrete barrier cubes and continue on the well-traveled railroad grade.

8.8 Pass two wildlife viewing platforms, one on the right and one on the left.

8.9 Pass under the powerlines. Note that the small trail to the right is a habitat trail for foot travel only.

9.3 Pass a footbridge that goes to a campsite on the right.

9.5 Follow the gravel road to the right across a bridge and out to New Hampshire 25. Turn to the right (east) and return to the ball park 100 yards down the road.

9.8 You are at the ball park.

Variation 3: Descend to the right and ride on New Hampshire 25 for 0.5 mile before regaining the railroad bed by climbing to the right. Continue as in Variation 2 from mile 6.9.

Meader (Wachipauka) Pond

[See map page 146]

Location: 20.4 miles west of Interstate 93, exit 26, in Warren.

Distance: 1.6-mile one way.

Time: 20 to 40 minutes.

Tread: 1.6-mile on jeep trail.

Aerobic level: Moderate.

Technical difficulty: 3- on jeep trail.

Highlights: A nice short ride through the forest to a charming little pond.

Land status: White Mountain National Forest.

Maps: WMNF Mountain Bike Map; DeLorme New Hampshire Atlas and Gazetteer, 10th edition; USGS Warren Quadrangle.

Access: From Interstate 93, take exit 26, turn onto New Hampshire 25 west (Tenney Mountain Highway), and go 4 miles to the rotary. Take the first right, following New Hampshire 25 for 15.8 miles to the town of Warren (0.5 mile past the fire station and rocket). Turn left onto Pine Hill Road and continue past a graveyard for 1.8 miles to the intersection with Swain Hill Road and Weeks Crossing. Stay left on Weeks Crossing Road (dirt) for 1.9 miles to Weeks Crossing Pond on the right. Park here or continue 0.4 mile as the road narrows and becomes rougher, to a clearing at the intersection of three logging roads. The left and right roads are blocked by boulders; park here. The ride begins as you climb up the center, more used-looking road.

The ride

0.0   Begin the moderate climb up the center jeep trail (the more used-looking road). Level 3-.

0.4   Continue climbing more steeply, staying right on the more worn road.

0.6   As the climb eases, ride straight through a four-way intersection with logging roads.

1.1   Stay to the left at this Y intersection and follow the arrow on the snowmobile sign. There are several very rough and muddy sections of trail that can easily be circumvented on auxiliary trails to the left and right.

1.6   Pass through a campsite and drop down to the pond's edge. Return by reversing the route.

Variation: This ride can easily be added as a side trip to extend the Warren–East Haverhill RR Grade ride (Ride 40).

BLUEBERRY MOUNTAIN TRAIL
Ride 42

TUNNEL BROOK TRAIL AND NORTH-SOUTH ROAD
Ride 43

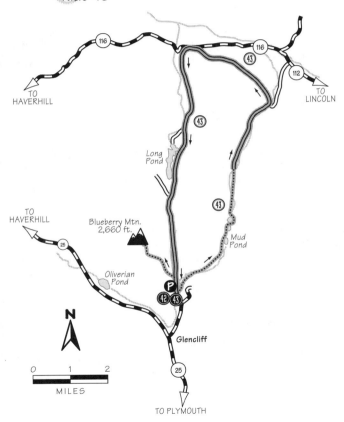

Blueberry Mountain Trail

Location: 25.9 miles west of Interstate 93, exit 26, in Benton.

Distance: 1.8-mile one way.

42—BLUBERRY MOUNTAIN TRAIL

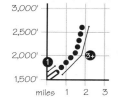

Time: 30 minutes to 1.5 hours.

Tread: 0.4 mile on jeep trail (Forest Service road); 1.4 miles on singletrack across granite ledge near the top.

Aerobic level: Strenuous.

Technical difficulty: 1 on Forest Service road; 3+ on singletrack, with some carries necessary going up the slabs.

Highlights: This ride gives you the feeling of being on one of the higher peaks in New Hampshire with subalpine vegetation and open spaces among many granite slabs. The climb is a brutal one, but the rewards are plenty. There are stunning views and great riding across some of that famous Granite State granite. The return ride is a hoot as you pick your way down the slabs and descend into the forest on technical but very rideable terrain. And it's downhill all the way to your car door!

Hazards: Use caution when this trail is wet, particularly on the slabs since they become very slippery. Stay on the marked path to minimize damage to the fragile plant life growing on the upper portion of this ride; and don't forget sunscreen. Unlike many rides in New Hampshire, this ride gets you out from under the trees and into the direct sun.

Land status: White Mountain National Forest.

Maps: WMNF Mountain Bike Map; DeLorme New Hampshire Atlas and Gazetteer, 10th edition; USGS East Haverhill Quadrangle.

Access: From Interstate 93, take exit 26, New Hampshire 25 west (Tenney Mountain Highway), and go 4 miles to the rotary. Take the first right, following New Hampshire 25 for 20.2 miles. Bear right onto High Street, the road going to the Glencliff Home for the Elderly, and go 1 mile to unpaved North-South Road; turn left. Notice the sign that says this is a fee area and parked vehicles must display a recreation pass. Also be aware that North-South Road is not maintained for winter travel and is closed from December to May. Go 0.7 mile and park at the Blueberry Mountain Trailhead on the left. The trail begins as you climb between the large boulders and over the dirt mound past the trail sign.

The ride

0.0   Ready your granny gear for a good workout. Climb between the large boulders and over the dirt mound, past the trail sign, up Forest Service Road 191—a wide, open, grassy road often covered in wildflowers. Level 1.

0.1   Bear left at a log landing, continuing to climb the grassy trail past several water bars.

0.2   Cross a water bar and diverge right from the comforts of the grassy Forest Service road climbing the steeper singletrack.

0.4   Cross a logging road, continuing on more technical singletrack. Level 3+.

0.7   Use caution climbing over a mossy and slippery rock outcrop.

0.8   Slippery when wet! Use caution on the more frequent ledge outcrops as you ascend into hemlock forest.

1.1 Ascend a steep, clean, granite slab marked with a yellow paint blaze and flanked by blueberry bushes. Look for paint blazes and rock cairns to assist you in navigating your way through the slab areas between here and the top. Note that the trees are becoming dwarfed as you continue to climb into more alpinelike terrain, past the many blueberry bushes that give this ride its name. Some carries may be necessary.

1.8 The climb eases and the trail ends at a large cairn sitting atop a slab surrounded by thick trees. Though there is no real view here, there are excellent views to be gained as you return on the same trail you worked so hard to climb up; enjoy them on your way down.

Tunnel Brook Trail and North-South Road

[See map page 152]

Location: 25.9 miles west of Interstate 93, exit 26, in Benton.

Distance: 17.2-mile loop.

Time: 1.5 to 2.5 hours.

Tread: 4.2 miles on ATV-width singletrack; 0.2 mile on jeep trail; 12.5 miles on dirt road; 0.3 mile on paved road.

Aerobic level: Strenuous.

Technical difficulty: 1 on jeep trail, dirt and paved road; 3 and 4 on ATV-width singletrack.

Highlights: Fun riding on the singletrack, and the ponds are very peaceful.

Hazards: Traffic on New Hampshire 116, bugs near ponds.

Land status: White Mountain National Forest, town roads.

Maps: WMNF Mountain Bike Map; DeLorme New Hampshire Atlas and Gazetteer, 10th edition; USGS East Haverhill and Mount Moosilauke quadrangles.

Access: From Interstate 93, take exit 26, New Hampshire 25 west (Tenney Mountain Highway), and go 4 miles to the rotary. Take the first right, following New Hampshire 25 for 20.2 miles. Bear right onto High Street, the road going to the Glencliff Home for the Elderly, and go 1 mile to North-South Road (unpaved); turn left. Note the sign that says this is a fee area and parked vehicles must display a recreation pass. Also be aware that North-South Road is not maintained for winter travel and is closed from December to May. Go 0.7 mile and park at the Blueberry Mountain Trailhead on the left. The ride begins as you exit the parking area, turn right, and ride south downhill on North-South Road.

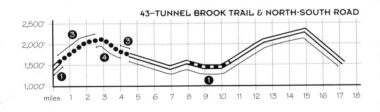

43—TUNNEL BROOK TRAIL & NORTH-SOUTH ROAD

The ride

0.0   Exit the parking area, turn right, and ride south downhill on North-South Road.

0.3   Turn hard left onto the Tunnel Brook Trail (grassy, centered jeep trail) by the trailhead signpost.

0.4   Pass a small camp on the right.

0.5   Cross the brook, continuing on ATV-width singletrack as you climb up the beautiful brookside with water cascading over mossy rocks. Level 3.

0.7   Traverse a side hill high over the stream below. Level 4.

0.9   Cross the two streams on rocks as they converge. Continue on easier trail.

1.3   Cross a stream and carry up the far bank.

1.5   Continue around the left of a small pond with a dam and a pump house back to the right. The trail climbs more steeply from here past a granite post by a land survey marker.

1.6   The trail, still deep in the forest, opens and becomes wider and grassy.

1.7   Carry over a small, deep streambed. Continue on beautiful trail.

2.2   The climb eases quite a bit as you enter hemlocks and approach Mud Pond.

2.6   Gain fine views of the very quaint Mud Pond, followed by a series of beaver ponds: prime moose-spotting terrain. In a clearing, pass a cairn topped by a blue stone.

2.7   Cross a marshy area and continue through a tunnel of young hemlock trees on smooth trail. They say where there's smoke there's fire; in New Hampshire, where there's water there are bugs! Hope you remembered your bug dope.

2.8   Pass a campsite on the pond's edge in the hemlocks and ride into more technical terrain with moss-covered rocks. Level 4.

3.0   Pass through birch trees as you descend slightly until you emerge at a stream crossing on the edge of Slide Pond (note the slide on the hillside). You will probably have to carry a small section as you work your way around the edge of this pond.

3.3 Pass a stone cairn and descend quickly to a stream crossing.

3.5 Pass a very neatly stacked cairn.

3.8 Bounce over a particularly root-infested section of trail.

4.0 Ride across this stream and continue on better trail. Level 3.

4.1 Ride across another stream to a section of bone-rattling boulders. The trail widens slightly and descends quickly, crossing several water bars.

4.7 Exit the woods and join a cul-de-sac leading to a dirt road. You can turn around here or return via the roads described below. Head down the road. If you're a speed junkie, you're gonna love this. Level 1.

4.8 Cross a bridge.

5.7 Go speeding past the Benton Trailhead to Mount Moosilauke.

7.2 Turn left onto Noxon Road, climbing moderately. Don't complain. Did you really think you could have a downhill run like that without some uphill?

7.9 The road becomes intermittently paved as you climb and descend.

10.0 Turn left onto New Hampshire 116.

10.3 Turn left onto North-South Road (not signposted; look for the sign to Long Pond and Glencliff) and begin climbing the dirt road.

10.4 Climb steadily past a green Forest Service gate.

12.0 Pass Forest Service Road 146.

12.2 You're teased by a descent before climbing again.

12.7 Pass Forest Service Road 19A to Long Pond on the right.

13.4 Catch a glimpse of Long Pond on the right. Rest while you can; the climb isn't over yet.

14.0 Are you playing "The top has got to be over the next rise"?

15.0 Forest Service Road 190 is on the right, and yes, you are at the top. You can safely shift out of the granny gears and begin a joyful, continuous descent. It's all downhill from here!

15.8 You probably didn't notice that bridge you just flew over.

16.9 Did you notice that bridge?

17.2 Don't miss the parking area and the end of the ride.

Ashland

The Ridgepole Trail

Location: 10 miles east of Interstate 93, exit 24, in Holderness.

Distance: 9-mile round trip.

Time: 2 to 3 hours.

Tread: 4.0 miles on incredible singletrack; 1.7 miles on arduous ATV-width doubletrack; 1.9 miles on jeep trail; 0.6 mile on dirt road; 0.8 mile on paved road.

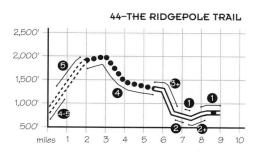

THE RIDGEPOLE TRAIL
Ride 44

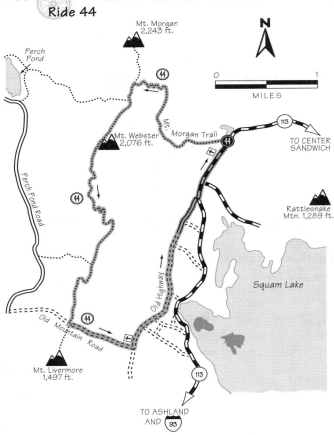

Mt. Morgan
2,243 ft.

Perch
Pond

N

0 _____ 1
MILES

44

Mt. Morgan Trail

Mt. Webster
2,076 ft.

113

TO CENTER
SANDWICH

44

44

Perch Pond Road

Rattlesnake
Mtn. 1,289 ft.

Old Highway

Squam Lake

44

Old Mountain Road

Mt. Livermore
1,497 ft.

113

TO ASHLAND
AND 93

Aerobic level: Strenuous for the initial 1.7-mile climb, then it's mostly an easy cruise.

Technical difficulty: 4 and 5 on singletrack; 4 to 5 on ATV-width doubletrack; 2, 2+, and 3+ on jeep trail; 1 on paved road.

Highlights: This is the most classic ride of the area. It begins with a grunt up the side of Mount Morgan. Once on the Ridgepole Trail, you traverse the top of the Squam Range to the west with views of Squam and Winnipesaukee lakes on some of the finest singletrack in the area. Descend wildly to old roads, passing beautiful estate farms.

Hazards: The Mount Morgan Trail is heavily used by hikers. Please be courteous to them.

Land status: Private lands with trails maintained by the Squam Lakes Association.

Maps: DeLorme New Hampshire Atlas and Gazetteer, 10th edition; USGS Squam Mountains Quadrangle.

Access: From Interstate 93, exit 24, go 4.5 miles south on U.S. Highway 3/New Hampshire 25 east, through Ashland (bear left at 0.7 mile). Turn east (left) onto New Hampshire 113 in Holderness, and go 5.5 miles. Slow down as you see the pedestrian sign and the speed limit drops to 25 mph. Park in the parking area on the left, at the top of the blind rise opposite the West Rattlesnake Mountain Trailhead. The ride begins as you pass the white gate at the back of the parking area on the Mount Morgan Trail.

The ride

0.0   Ride past the white gate with a yellow sign on it for the Mount Morgan Trail (at the back of the parking area). Follow well-worn, ATV-width doubletrack trail, climbing over roots. Level 4 to 5.

0.3 Cross a series of footbridges, traversing an area that is often muddy.

0.5 You get a break in the climb on more level terrain.

0.7 Climb steeply through rocks on the first of several short Level 5 sections.

0.9 Another short section of difficult rocky trail. Level 5.

1.3 Climb, or carry, very rocky singletrack as the trail, if you can believe it, gets steeper! Level 5.

1.5 You're probably wondering why you even bothered to bring a bike (resembling an expensive walking stick at this point), but you will know soon enough.

1.7 As the trail reaches the top of a rise, your disposition is guaranteed to improve as you proceed to a trail junction marked by yellow signs. A side trip of 0.4 mile to the summit of Mount Morgan is well worth your time. Stash your bike in the woods and catch the excellent view of the lakes region, including Lakes Squam and Winnipesaukee, from the rocky summit. To continue with the ride, go west (left) from the intersection, following the Crawford Ridgepole Trail toward Old Mountain Road and Mount Livermore on narrow, undulating singletrack. You soon cross a very rocky section and drop down into a boggy area with grass. Level 5.

1.9 After crossing a second marshy section, the trail becomes less rocky and a lot more fun. Level 4.

2.1 Pass the Cascade Trail (unmarked), which descends to the right.

3.2 Catch a glimpse of Squam Lake through the trees on the left before a fantastic, fast, and twisty downhill pitch.

3.6 Check out the great view of the lakes from a ledge at the end of this short trail on the left. Hold on! Begin a major descent through a long series of steep, sharp, and really fun switchbacks.

4.2 Another view of the lakes on the left.

4.7 Pass through an opening in a beautiful stone wall.

5.2 Cross an old skidder trail and follow it as it bends left at a stone wall.

5.3 Descend a steep, side-sloping switchback and cross an intermittent stream.

5.4 Cross an intermittent stream on neatly stacked rocks.

5.6 As you gradually climb, cross an old skidder trail.

5.7 At a four-way junction, turn left on Old Mountain Road, a wide jeep trail that is washed out in some places, and descend to the Old Highway. Level 3+.

6.2 Make a worthwhile side trip into the field for a look down to the lake. Poke around for an old house foundation behind the wall at the top of the field.

6.4 Stay left as you join the Old Highway. Descend past a stone wall lined with sugar maples overlooking Squam Lake. Level 2.

6.5 Pass the Carr Cemetery on the left.

6.7 Pass a sugar shack and join paved road, riding past Burleigh Farm Road on the right. Level 1.

6.8 Ride past the farmhouse and join a sand and gravel jeep trail. In 40 yards, bear right, away from the paved driveway, descending past a crabapple tree. Level 2+.

7.1 Cross a water bar.

7.2 Continue past jeep trails on both sides as you begin a short, steep climb on slightly washed-out trail.

7.4 Pass a farmhouse on the right.

7.5 Climb on loose rock past a field access road on the left.

7.6 Crest a rise between stone walls and descend.

7.7 Join dirt road past driveways on the left and right. Level 1.

8.0 Pass driveways and ride in front of the John True farmhouse and its white picket fence.

8.3 Stay left as you descend to New Hampshire 113 (paved) and climb steadily to the parking area.

9.0 Turn left into the parking area.

Bridgewater
Mountain Loop

Location: 3.9 miles west of Interstate 93, exit 24, in Bridgewater.

Distance: 11.7-mile loop.

Time: 2 to 3 hours.

Tread: 2.8 miles on ATV-width doubletrack; 2.8 miles on jeep trail; 6.1 miles on dirt road.

Aerobic level: Strenuous.

Technical difficulty: 2 and 3 on ATV-width doubletrack; 3 and 5 on jeep trail; 2 on dirt road.

Highlights: This is the ride for those of you who love long, steep climbs and screamingly fast downhills. The phrase "good training ride" comes to mind. The road portions of this ride are absolutely beautiful and offer outstanding views. The off-road is really fun and challenging.

Land status: Private land and town roads.

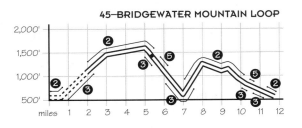

BRIDGEWATER MOUNTAIN LOOP
Ride 45

JACKSON POND LOOP
Ride 46

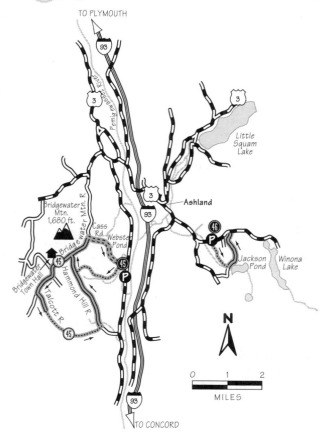

TO PLYMOUTH

93

3

Pemigewasset River

3

Little Squam Lake

3

93

Ashland

Bridgewater Mtn. 1,680 ft.

Cass Rd.

Bridge Water Mtn. R.

Webster Pond

46

P

Jackson Pond

Winona Lake

Bridgewater Town Hall

45

P

45

Hammond Hill R.

Talcott R.

45

N

0   1   2
MILES

93

TO CONCORD

Maps: DeLorme New Hampshire Atlas and Gazetteer, 10th edition; USGS Holderness Quadrangle.

Access: From Interstate 93, exit 24, turn north on U.S. Highway 3/New Hampshire 25 west, and go 1.4 miles. Turn left onto Depot Street and go 0.3 mile to the stop sign. Turn south (left) and go 2.2 miles on River Road to Sawhegenet Falls Park Recreation Area on the left. Park in the few spaces on River Road under the black-and-white park sign, or drive down to additional parking in the park. The ride begins on the west side of River Road, across from the black-and-white park sign. Look for a snowmobile trail, gated with a cable, that enters the woods under the utility lines.

The ride

0.0 The ride begins on the west side of River Road, across from the black-and-white park sign. Look for a snow-mobile trail, gated with a cable, that enters the woods under the utility lines. Pass around the cable and ride ATV-width doubletrack on a pine-needle base. Level 2.

0.1 Stay right at this trail junction. Don't miss this turn on the way back.

0.2 Follow the trail around the southeast edge of Webster Pond.

0.5 Cross straight through a four-way intersection. You will be returning on the trail to the right (Cass Road).

0.6 Pass a trail on the left.

0.7 Stay right initially, and in 15 yards go on the center trail (straight past a trail to the right).

0.8 Cross a small wooden bridge and begin a steady, moderate climb along the edge of Great Brook on mostly good trail with some difficult spots. Level 3.

1.2 Cross a small bridge.

1.4	Follow the trail as it turns left across an intermittent stream, and follow the barbed-wire fence.
1.6	Traverse a mud hole with logs and rocks.
2.1	The trail bends left, wraps around the knoll, and descends.
2.3	Turn right onto Hammond Hill Road and climb moderately on the dirt road. You will see this section of road again. Level 2.
2.4	Go left at the intersection and left again as you join Bridgewater Hill Road.
2.5	Pass a spring on the right before beginning a short, steep climb.
2.7	Crest the climb and descend a bit.
2.9	Pass the Old Home Cemetery on the left.
3.1	Pass the Bridgewater Town Hall on the right; as the road bends left, still climbing, pass a road on the right.
3.3	Stay right at this intersection, by a little red house on the left following the sign to Bristol.
4.8	At the top of that very steep climb, take a moment to enjoy the view across the field on the right. You can get a glimpse of Newfound Lake to the west.
4.9	Just as you begin to descend, turn left onto Talcott Road (sign posted on the left). Climb steeply up this unmaintained road.
5.3	Take a roller-coaster ride, undulating steeply down old pavement through the woods.
5.5	Pass a wooden gate on the right and continue on jeep trail with a grassy center. Level 3.
5.7	Pass a wooden gate on the right. As the trail bends left, descend steeply through a rocky, washed-out section. Level 5.
5.9	Climb a short hill on improving trail.
6.1	Descend another steep, washed-out section of trail.
6.2	Ride grassy trail again. Level 3.

6.3 Pass a snowmobile trail on the right and descend on smooth, fast trail.

6.5 Cross an intermittent stream and continue descending on badly washed-out trail. Level 5.

7.0 The trail improves for a short distance after a deep water bar at the base of a steep drop.

7.1 You're probably going pretty fast now, so you'll want to use caution as you come around a sharp right bend into one last section of washed-out trail. The trail really does get better from here. Level 3.

7.3 Turn left as you join a gravel driveway and left again as you join Hammond Hill Road (dirt). Level 2.

7.4 Cross a bridge over Woodman Brook and begin a l-o-n-g, strenuous grunt climb. Yes, this is going to hurt.

8.2 You made it: the top of the climb. Let it rip on the descent!

8.8 Cross Great Brook on a wooden bridge, and get ready to climb again. Sorry, the climbing is not over yet.

9.0 Pass the trail you rode in on to the right. You're on familiar ground now.

9.1 Stay right this time, joining Bridgewater Hill Road in the opposite direction.

9.2 Pass a red house with white trim on the left that hosts an excellent view north to Franconia Notch. Begin descending, passing another farm with a good view on the left.

9.7 As the road flattens and begins to gradually climb, look for Cass Road (unmarked; it looks a bit like a driveway on the right). It begins climbing gradually along a stone wall on the left edge of a long, narrow field, posted "No Trespassing."

10.1 Continue straight across logging roads to the left and right at the top of the rise. Begin a long descent all the way back to Webster Pond.

10.2 Pass a driveway to the left and a gate to a grassy field to the right. The trail narrows to jeep trail and continues descending. Level 3.

10.3 Descend washed-out, overgrown trail. Level 5.

10.5 Pass a trail on the left. Continue descending on dirt and loose gravel. Level 3.

10.8 Pass a faint logging road on the right.

11.2 At the four-way intersection by Webster Pond, which you passed through at 0.5 mile, turn left onto the soft ATV-width doubletrack. Proceed around the pond and follow the same route back to the start. Level 2.

11.6 Don't miss this left turn.

11.7 Pass around the cable and onto River Road. If you're hot and nasty, try a swim in the Pemi River down in Sawhegenet Falls Park Recreation Area.

Jackson Pond Loop

[See Map page 165]

Location: 2.1 miles east of Interstate 93, exit 24, in New Hampton.

Distance: 2.9-mile loop.

Time: 30 to 45 minutes.

Tread: 0.2 mile on singletrack; 1.1 miles on jeep trail; 0.9 mile on dirt road; 0.7 mile on paved road.

Aerobic level: Moderate.

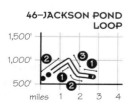

Technical difficulty: 2 on singletrack; 2 and 3 on jeep trail; 1 and 2 on dirt road; 1 on paved road.

Highlights: A splendid ride through forest and past Jackson Pond.

Land status: Private and town roads.

Maps: DeLorme New Hampshire Atlas and Gazetteer, 10th edition; USGS Holderness Quadrangle.

Access: From Interstate 93, exit 24, go south 0.7 mile on U.S. Highway 3/New Hampshire 25 east. Veer right onto New Hampshire 132 south in Ashland by Cumberland Farms. Go 0.1 mile and veer left onto Winona Road just past the Ashland Fire Station. Go 1.3 miles (0.5 mile past Dana Hill Road) and park on the right in the small parking area by a utility building surrounded by a chain-link fence. Look closely for the parking area, before a cable guardrail, just as the road climbs, bending right then left past a straight, flat section on Winona Road. The ride begins along the railroad tracks at the back of the parking area.

The ride

0.0 Ride out the back of the parking area and up onto the railroad tracks. Go left, following the tracks; the riding is easiest on the right side. Level 2.

0.1 Turn right across a small stream, climbing into the mossy pine forest on singletrack. There is often a wooden pallet in the stream, to aid your crossing. In 50 yards, pass through a fallen stone wall and stay left on jeep trail as you join an old roadbed. Follow the old road as it switches back sharply to the right, at an old bridge abutment, and begins a gradual climb.

0.6   Stay left at the trail junction, following more worn jeep trail. (Or descend to the right a short distance to a very attractive small pond at a concrete dam, a nice rest spot.)

0.9   The trail ascends a small rise to the left and becomes more grassy.

1.0   Stay left onto Jackson Pond Road (dirt) as you approach Jackson Pond. The road follows the north shore for some distance. Level 1.

1.3   The road bends to the left, away from the pond, and climbs moderately.

1.5   Crest the hill and descend, staying left at a driveway on the right.

1.6   Continue past the end of the maintained road onto jeep trail descending into the woods. Stay right of the "Pass at Your Own Risk, Class VI Road" sign. Level 3.

1.8   Stay right, continuing to descend at the Y intersection on overgrown, washed-out trail until you come out in less than 0.1 mile, staying right on greatly improved grassy road.

1.9   Stay right past a tall, skinny, wooden building and descend on dirt road. Level 2.

2.1   Cross over the railroad tracks on a large wooden bridge.

2.2   Turn left onto Winona Road (paved). Level 1.

2.9   Turn left into the parking area.

A Short Index of Rides

Sweet Singletrack Rides
(may include road and doubletrack portions)
3. Kancamagus Race Course
8. Cilley Mountain Loop
22. Atwood Trail
28. Brown Ash Swamp
30. East Ponds Loop
33. Greeley Ponds Trail
42. Blueberry Mountain Trail
44. The Ridgepole Trail

Great Climbs—The Yearn to Burn
4. To the View Trail
5. Bog Brook Eddy
7. Gordon Pond Trail
15. Chandler Hill Road
31. Livermore Road
32. Timber Camp Trail
38. Groton Hollow
42. Blueberry Mountain Trail
44. The Ridgepole Trail
45. Bridgewater Mountain Loop

The Need for Speed
4. To the View Trail (on return)
7. Gordon Pond Trail (on return)
9. Ellsworth Pond to Forest Service Road 348
   to Forest Service Road 112
16. Chandler Hill Power Run
22. Atwood Trail
31. Livermore Road (on return)
32. Timber Camp Trail (on return)
38. Groton Hollow (on return)
42. Blueberry Mountain Trail (on return)
44. The Ridgepole Trail

Cruising the Countryside
1. Franconia Notch Bike Path
2. Lincoln Woods Trail

12. East Rumney–Campton Bog Road
17. Sandwich Notch Road
18. Beebe River Road
34. Tripoli Road
39. Plymouth-Rumney RR Grade
40. Warren-East Haverhill RR Grade

Technical Tests
7. Gordon Pond Trail
8. Cilley Mountain Loop
19. Flat Mountain Pond
22. Atwood Trail
28. Brown Ash Swamp
30. East Ponds Loop
33. Greeley Ponds Trail
42. Blueberry Mountain Trail
44. The Ridgepole Trail

Epic Rides—The Long Haul
8. Cilley Mountain Loop
18. Beebe River Road
19. Flat Mountain Pond
37. Plymouth Mountain Loop
43. Tunnel Brook Trail and North-South Road
44. The Ridgepole Trail
45. Bridgewater Mountain Loop

Appendix A
Other Riding Areas

This appendix lists other riding areas in the state that offer excellent mountain biking. Some are near, and some are far. With the snow gone from the slopes of your favorite ski hill and your skis and snowboards packed away for the summer, remember that the fun doesn't have to be over. Ever increasing in popularity is a new aspect of the mountain-biking sport: lift-service biking. Below are some of the New Hampshire ski section is of state parks that offer trail riding.

Ski Areas

Bretton Woods Summer Park
Bretton Woods, NH
603-278-5000

25 lift-serviced trails and 20 kilometers of cross-country trails open to mountain bikers. There are two terrain gardens to challenge yourself on, as well as a duel slalom course.

Cranmore
North Conway, NH
603-356-5543

Lift-serviced riding with challenging terrain for intermediate and advanced riders on wide-open slopes and singletrack trails. Rentals are available at the full-service mountain-bike shop.

Franconia Village Touring Center
Franconia, NH
603-823-5542

The touring center offers 12 kilometers of beginner-to-intermediate mountain-bike terrain at no charge.

Great Glen Trails at Mount Washington
Pinkham Notch, NH
603-466-2333

12 kilometers of beginner-to-intermediate riding. Bike rentals are available, as well as full-moon tours.

Gunstock
Gilford, NH
603-293-4341

Gunstock's cross-country trails (as well as selected trails on the mountain) are open to riders. Gunstock has bike rentals, but no lifit service.

Loon Mountain Park
Kancamagus Highway
Lincoln, New Hampshire
603-745-6281, ext. 5463

2,100 vertical feet of challenging downhill terrain accessible via a 1.5-mile mountain skyride. There are also more than 35 kilometers of cross-country trails available at the base of the mountain. The Mountain Bike Pro Shop offers a full range of rentals, sales, repairs, and guided tours in the Loon area. A shuttle bus is available to transport riders.

Mount Sunapee
Mount Sunapee, NH
603-763-2356

Lift-serviced trails for beginner to intermediate riders on the mountain. Rides around scenic Lake Sunapee and on local country roads are also available.

Waterville Valley
Base Camp Adventure Center
Town Square
Waterville Valley, NH 03215
603-236-8311
www.waterville.com

Riders can venture out on 30 miles of patrolled trails for every level of ability. The Snow's Mountain chairlift will take you to the 2,090-foot summit for easy access to a variety of terrain; it offers great views of the valley and surrounding White Mountain National Forest. A one-hour self-guided tour departs from the summit. Guided tours and rentals are available as well. Check into the Base Camp at the Town Square for trail-pass information and current fees.

Woodbound Inn
62 Woodbound Road
Rindge, NH 03461
603-532-8341

15 kilometers of mountain-bike trails for riders of all abilities with the purchase of a trail pass.

Best State Parks for Biking

Many of the state parks and trails are open to mountain-bike use, though some are closed for safety or environmental concerns. Trails closed for mountain biking are signed with a "No Bikes" symbol. Most trails are closed for the "mud season" in the spring. Mount Monadnock State Park, home to the second most-hiked mountain in the world, is closed to mountain bikes.

Bear Brook State Park, located in Allenstown, just off New Hampshire 28, has good riding opportunities for mountain bikers.

The park has nearly 10,000 acres and is heavily forested, with an elaborate trail system. Overnight camping is available. For more information and trail maps, call Bear Brook State Park at 603-485-9874.

Pawtuckaway State Park, located in Nottingham and Raymond, is located 3.5 miles north of the junction of New Hampshire Routes 101 and 156 and has trails open to mountain bikes. This 5,600-acre park offers overnight camping for individuals and organized groups. For more information and trail maps, call Pawtuckaway State Park at 603-895-3031.

Pisgah State Park, located in Winchester, Chesterfield, and Hinsdale, off New Hampshire 63, includes over 13,500 acres of rough, forested terrain. The area's 21 square miles make it the largest property in the New Hampshire state park system. For information and trail maps, call 603-239-8153.

Day-use Areas

Popular day-use areas for mountain biking include the **Hopkinton-Everett Recreation Area,** the **Rockingham Recreational Trail,** and the **Sugar River Recreational Trail**. For more information on these and other trail opportunities not covered in this guide, contact the White Mountain National Forest, Supervisor's Office, Laconia, New Hampshire 03246; 603-528-8721.

Other Areas

The Beaver Brook Association's conservation land in Hollis has trails varying from easy to difficult. There are several trailhead parking areas on Proctor Hill Road (New Hampshire 130) west of the town's center. A map is available from the association.

Areas to Be Avoided

Rattlesnake Mountain: Please **do not ride** this trail. Feel free to hike it, however. It is a fantastic short trail with stunning views of Squam Lake. Heavy use by hikers just doesn't make biking the trail safe.

Appendix B

Services and Information

Bike Shops and Guide Services

The Base Camp
1 Ski Area Road
Waterville Valley, NH 03215
603-236-4666

The Greasy Wheel Bike Shop
40 South Main Street
Plymouth, NH 03264
603-536-3655

Rhino Bike Works
95 Main Street
Plymouth NH 03264
603-536-3919

Riverside Cycles
4 Riverside Drive
Ashland, NH 03217
603-968-9676

Ski Fanatics
Route 49
Campton, NH 03223
603-726-4327

White Mountain Cyclists
Main Street/ P.O. Box 902
Lincoln, NH 03251
603-745-8852
Tours and shuttles available.

Information Sources

Appalachian Mountain Club
5 Joy Street
Boston, MA 02108
(617) 523-0636

**Pemigewasset
District Ranger**
RFD 3, Box 15
Route 175
Plymouth, NH 03264
603-536-1310

**The New England Mountain
Bike Association (NEMBA)**
P.O. Box 380557
Cambridge, MA 02238
(607) 354-7050 or 1-800-57NEMBA

**New Hampshire Division of
Parks and Recreation**
Bureau of Trails
P.O. Box 1856
Concord, NH 03302-1856
(603) 271-3254
Fax: (603) 271-2629

**The New Hampshire
Mountain Bike Association**
Paul Mikalaoskas
Highland Street
Ashland, NH 032217
(603) 968-7840

**Plymouth Chamber
of Commerce**
20 Highland Street
P.O. Box 65
Plymouth, NH 03264
(603) 536-1001

Squam Lakes Association
Route 3
Holderness, NH 03245
(603) 968-7336

**U.S. Department of
Agriculture**
Forest Service
White Mountain
National Forest
Supervisor's Office
Laconia, NH 03246
(603) 528-8721

Appendix C
Campgrounds

The following are White Mountain National Forest campgrounds close to the Pemigewasset Valley rides. Brochures listing services, fees, and complete information can be obtained from the local ranger stations or by calling the White Mountain National Forest supervisor's office at 603-528-8721, TTY: 603-528-8722. You can also write to 719 N. Main Street, Laconia, NH 03246.

Reservations can be made only by calling the National Reservations Center at 1-800-280-CAMP(2267). Do not call the White Mountain National Forest for reservations. Hours of operation are Monday through Friday, excluding holidays:

January 5 to May 15 .... 9 A.M.–4 P.M.
May 18 to September 4 .... 9 A.M.–7 P.M.
(Saturday) .... 9 A.M.–4 P.M.
September 7 to October 2 .... 9 A.M.–4 P.M.

National Forest Camping Areas

Big Rock
Kancamagus Highway
(6 miles east of Lincoln)
603-536-1310
TTY: 603-536-3281
Open year-round.

Campton Family and Group
New Hampshire Route 49
Campton, NH 03223
603-536-1310
or 1-800-380-2267
TTY: 603-536-3281
or 1-800-879-4496
Open mid-April to mid-October.

Hancock
Kancamagus Highway (12.5 miles west of Conway)
603-536-1310
TTY: 603-536-3281
Open year-round.

Jigger Johnson
Kancamagus Highway
(12.5 miles west of Conway)
603-447-5448
TTY: 603-447-1989
Open late May to mid-October.

Passaconaway
Kancamagus Highway
(12.5 miles west of Conway)
603-447-5448
TTY: 603-447-1989
Open mid-May to
mid-October.

Russell Pond
Tripoli Road (3.7 miles
off Interstate 93,
exit 31, Campton)
603-536-1310
TTY: 603-536-3281
Open mid-May to
mid-October.

Waterville
(8 miles northeast on
New Hampshire 49 from
Interstate 93, exit 28, Waterville)
(603) 536-1310
TTY: (603) 536-3281
Open year-round, winter
walk-in access only.

Wildwood
(New Hampshire 112,
7 miles west of Lincoln)
(603) 869-2626
TTY: (603) 869-3104
Open mid-May to
mid-December.

There is also camping available in Tripoli Road Dispersed Camping Area. Camping is permitted on the south side of Tripoli Road. Vehicles must have a valid parking permit or face towing. A brochure is available. Check with the Pemigewasset Ranger District, RFD 3 Box 15, Route 175, Plymouth, NH 03264, 603-536-1310.

Glossary

ATB: All-terrain bicycle; a.k.a. mountain bike, sprocket rocket, fat tire flyer.

ATV: All-terrain vehicle; in this book ATV refers to motorbikes and three- and four-wheelers designed for off-road use.

Bail: Getting off the bike, usually in a hurry, and whether or not you meant to. Often a last resort.

Bunny hop: Leaping up, while riding, and lifting both wheels off the ground to jump over an obstacle (or for sheer joy).

Clamper cramps: That burning, cramping sensation experienced in the hands during extended braking.

Clean: To ride without touching a foot (or other body part) to the ground; to ride a tough section successfully.

Clipless: A type of pedal with a binding that accepts a special cleat on the soles of bike shoes. The cleat clicks in for more control and efficient pedaling and out for safe landings (in theory).

Contour: A line on a topographic map showing a continuous elevation level over uneven ground. Also used as a verb to indicate a fairly easy or moderate grade: "The trail contours around the canyon rim before the final grunt to the top."

Dab: To put a foot or hand down (or hold onto or lean on a tree or other support) while riding. If you have to dab, then you haven't ridden that piece of trail **clean.**

Downfall: Trees that have fallen across the trail.

Doubletrack: A trail, jeep road, ATV route, or other track with two distinct ribbons of **tread,** typically with grass growing in between. No matter which side you choose, the other rut always looks smoother.

Endo: Lifting the rear wheel off the ground and riding (or abruptly not riding) on the front wheel only. Also known, at various degrees of control and finality, as a nose wheelie, "going over the handlebars," and a face plant.

Fall line: The angle and direction of a slope; the **line** you follow when gravity is in control and you aren't.

Graded: When a gravel road is scraped level to smooth out the washboards and potholes, it has been graded. In this book, a road is listed as graded only if it is regularly maintained. Not all such roads are graded every year, however.

Granny gear: The lowest (easiest) gear, a combination of the smallest of the three chainrings on the bottom bracket spindle (where the pedals and crank arms attach to the bike's frame) and the largest cog on the rear cluster. Shift down to your granny gear for serious climbing.

Hammer: To ride hard; derived from how it feels afterward: "I'm hammered."

Hammerhead: Someone who actually enjoys feeling **hammered.** A Type-A personality rider who goes hard and fast all the time.

Kelly hump: An abrupt mound of dirt across the road or trail. These are common on old logging roads and skidder tracks, placed there to block vehicle access. At high speeds, they become launching pads for bikes and inadvertent astronauts.

Line: The route (or trajectory) between or over obstacles or through turns. **Tread** or trail refers to the ground you're riding on; the line is the path you choose within the tread (and exists mostly in the eye of the beholder).

Off-the-seat: Moving your butt behind the bike seat and over the rear tire; used for control on extremely steep descents. This position increases braking power, helps prevent **endos,** and reduces skidding.